⚡ Daughter

Book II: Only in America

by Marlena Berlin
and Gaetano Catelli

Photo Credits

Marlena Berlin collection: front cover photos, upper right — Marlena's father, Werner, in WW II; upper left — her mother, Nina, during Marlena's infancy; bottom — Marlena, c. 1987. Rear cover photo — Marlena, c. 2010. Interior photos — pp. iii, ix, 1, 22, 25.

Gaetano Catelli Studios: pp. xiii, xiv, 4, 9, 15, 16, 18, 19, 40, 41, 42, 43, 45, 49, 51, 84, 100, 169.

Fonts

𝔓𝔩𝔞𝔦𝔫 𝔊𝔢𝔯𝔪𝔞𝔫𝔦𝔠𝔞, Bookman Old Style, Times New Roman, Arial.

ISBN-10: 0692118993
ISBN-13: 978-0692118993

To father and mother.

My parents on their wedding day in 1956.

Contents

Foreword to Book I

What follows is a true account of my life, to the best of my recollection. Of course, I cannot remember the exact words I spoke and heard decades ago. And, until I came to America, all the words were in High German (when I was conversing with father) or in the local dialect (when I was speaking with anyone else in South Tyrol, Italy, which is where I grew up). But the words I've placed in quotation marks capture, as well as I'm able to remember, the truth of what was said. My inner thoughts, likewise as best as I can recall them, appear in italics.

Statements about the historical context that shaped my parents, and indirectly me, are based mainly on entries in Wikipedia or on family lore. They are not meant to be a definitive historical account, but rather my subjective understanding of how my upbringing was affected by broader social currents.

Some chapters are arranged chronologically; others are arranged by topic. Inevitably, there's some overlap, and so a certain amount of repetition is required to ensure clarity.

Because of the sensitive nature of the material, it has taken me a long time to decide to write this memoir. For the sake of discretion, all of the names of people (including mine), places, and things have been changed, except for the names of countries, large cities, public figures, and a few well known consumer brands.

My hope is that readers of this book may gain increased confidence that with hard work, and competent and compassionate help, they or their loved ones can overcome even extremely difficult life circumstances.

Namaste,

Marlena Berlin
Queens, New York, 2015

Foreword to Book II

This volume deals with matters even more sensitive than those discussed in the 1st book. I hope my friends and family, and you the reader, will forgive me for my shortcomings.

Prologue to Book I

... I shall die more easily when I have finished writing this story. I have no right to call myself one who knows. I was one who seeks, and I still am. But, I no longer seek in the stars or in books — I'm beginning to hear the teachings of my blood pulsing within me. My story isn't pleasant. It's not sweet and harmonious like invented stories. It tastes of folly and bewilderment, of madness and dreams — like the life of all people who no longer want to lie to themselves. (*Demian,* Hermann Hesse)

I'm 5 years old, sitting in the back of my parents' Mercedes sedan, in the spring of 1964. My father, Werner, and my mother, Nina, are shouting at each other, as they often do. I'm leaning forward, trying to absorb what they are yelling, as I often do. I'm feeling anxious and scared. Things don't seem right — they feel dangerous.

Suddenly, mother tells father to stop the car. Elegantly dressed and made up, as always, she exits wearing her camel's hair coat, with an umbrella in one hand and a suitcase in the other. Her high heels tap-tap-tap on the wet pavement of a cold and rainy night in Munich, Germany, as I watch her walk away from her marriage to father and her responsibilities as a mother to me.

She's abandoning me to be raised solely by father, who spent World War II as a soldier in Adolf Hitler's *Waffen*-SS, and whose main regret about the war is that Germany *lost.*

Father is tall, still handsome in middle age, always finely dressed, and possessed of a commanding presence. He's quite generous with women — myself included. But, he's also a womanizer who quotes from the most sexist passages of Schopenhauer and Nietzsche, and cites Hitler, *approvingly*, as justification for his beliefs and behaviors.

At home he drinks heavily, and is often sexually predatory. He's an absolute tyrant who will brook no dissent, and has a violent and unpredictable temper, resulting in my often being assaulted physically and psychologically. In my early teens, I become a heroin addict to deaden my pain.

Father and I, early 1960's.

In 1980, when I'm 21, I inherit all of father's properties, which are worth several million dollars in today's money. In under 3 years, my inheritance is lost to my heroin habit, and to "friends of the family" who prove untrustworthy. In 1983, I arrive in America with a few dollars, 2 small sons, an 8th grade education, and a 1-oz. packet of heroin.

To this day, in spite of everything, I still love father — the one person in my life who never abandoned me. Since his death, I have spent my life trying to find him again.

Prologue to Book II

[Excerpted from Book I]

Fear of Homelessness

I'm on my own again, without any financial help. Christmas is coming in a few weeks, and since my then-partner Carlos hasn't gotten paid while he's in drug rehab (successfully, thank goodness), I've fallen 3 months behind in my rent.

I go to the New York City welfare department to get help with food and rent. They tell me the best they can do is put me and my sons into a shelter for the homeless. The thought of going into a shelter as a single mom with 2 young children (especially in the New York City of 1989) is really frightening to me.

Carlos returns from rehab in early 1990, and starts going to Alcoholics Anonymous and Narcotics Anonymous meetings. He gets a "sponsor" (someone with long-term abstinence who helps a newcomer), works "the 12 Steps", and remains clean and sober. I don't want to hurt Carlos, because he doesn't deserve to be hurt. He's always treated me well. I tell him I'm really happy that he's in recovery.

For his sake, I stay with him a little while longer, but I can't continue to live with him. I desperately want out. Since I don't want Carlos to relapse, I try to be gentle when I tell him I need to be free. He's very saddened at this turn of events, but fortunately he doesn't go back to using cocaine.

In February 1990, Carlos moves out and gets an apartment of his own. He still wants to see if our relationship can be mended, but I felt like a caged animal when we lived together. I feel so much better, and so much freer, living on my own again. There's no going back.

When I was still using heroin, I was tamping down the feelings of anger and rage that were bubbling below the surface. Once I get clean and dry, my emotions emerge at their full strength, especially my anger. I've felt a certain amount of rage since I was a child, but I had no idea just how much fury I've had inside of me all this time.

Carlos continues to want to marry me. He's a good man, but I can't endure him anymore. It's not just Carlos; it now happens with every man I date. I become furious if any man tries to get physically or even emotionally close to me. I have moments when I want to strangle whichever man I'm with at that moment.

Now that I'm free, I don't want to go back to depending on a man for support. I say to myself, *There's so much money in this city that there's got to be a better way. I can't live with a man, but my sons and I can't continue living in poverty either — it's just too hard.*

Viva Devorah

Agora Training

Back in 1988, soon after I broke up with Joe (discussed below), but before I started dating Carlos, I meet Najar when I'm doing real estate work. Najar is in his late 30's and quite handsome. Besides buying and selling residential and commercial properties, he has a carpet store on Broadway in the West 20's, and a nearby apartment where he stays.

We start dating. It's nothing serious, but he's the one who tells me about Agora Training, that it's changed his life, and that I should try it. He even offers to help me with the fee.

Agora Training takes place over the course of 2 weekends. The program is basically about paying attention to the "conversations" in my head: whether they are positive or negative, constructive or destructive, focused on a goal or merely idle thoughts. I learn to consciously shift from negative thoughts to positive ones. To establish clear expectations regarding what it is I want in my life — rather than to passively allow things to unfold on their own.

At the end of the training, we're asked to write out our goals — to create a short-term vision and a long-term vision for our life. I remember writing that I want to go back to school and get a GED, then go on to college and grad school, and someday become a psychotherapist. Even though I'm not making enough money to properly feed myself and my sons, I feel *there must be a way.*

While at Agora Training I meet Dinah, a very sweet woman. We become friends. I share with her that I'm in recovery from drug abuse. In turn, she shares that her adult daughter, Devorah, is using cocaine.

At Dinah's request, I soon meet Devorah. She's living in an abusive relationship with David, a used car dealer in Elmhurst. Besides selling cars from a lot in Queens, David deals cocaine. The 2 of them are using heavily, but I like Devorah, and we become good friends.

Thanksgiving, Christmas, and Easter

Sometime after Carlos enters rehab in late 1989, I go grocery shopping with my sons, Lukas and Johan. I don't have cash, but I do have a credit card. However, when we get to the checkout counter, my purchase is declined because I've reached my credit limit. My boys are scared and confused, since we have to leave a whole shopping cart of food at the store — and return home with nothing.

Not long afterward, Devorah comes by for a visit. When I open my refrigerator to get her some juice, she exclaims, "You have no food!"

Seeing how embarrassed and downcast I am, she then says, "Don't worry about it — we're going to Pathmark" (a local supermarket).

Devorah takes me and my sons there and spends $100 on food for us (a cart-full at the time). It's been a long while since I could buy that much food at one time. It feels like Thanksgiving, Christmas, and Easter all rolled into one.

I ask her, "You have so much money. What are you *doing?!*"

She answers, "Oh, no big deal. A little bit of kissy, kissy. Then f***, f***, f*** for a minute. I close my eyes, it's over and done with — and I have $100."

Christmas crèche, St. Anthony of Padua Church, NYC.

I'm like, "What are you talking about?"

She replies, "I'm working at a massage parlor."

My 1st thought is, *How gross!*

But then I have a moment of clarity: How much worse could it be than how my life is now? I've made many attempts to get work that would support myself and my sons — making pizzas and calzones, retail sales, real estate, cooking for Catholic priests in a seminary, driving for a car service, and cleaning homes.

For awhile I had a 2nd job, delivering *The New York Daily News* to homes in Queens. I'd leave my house at 3 AM, return at 6 AM, get my sons ready for school, and then leave for my day job. (Sometimes little Lukas would help me deliver the paper on weekends.) But I *still* haven't been able feed my 2 sons properly.

I think about times when I had such an excruciating toothache that I felt like hitting my head against the wall — but I couldn't afford to go to a dentist. And, about all the years we've been living without health insurance, leaving me unable to take my sons or myself for medical checkups.

The Bowery, NYC.

And now, I'm facing imminent eviction and the possibility of having to live with my boys in a New York City homeless shelter. I realize that if there were ever a dilemma that calls for a *Plan B,* this is it.

I ask Devorah for the phone number of the place where she works. She hesitates, but then gives me the number of a friend of hers who knows people in the business.

Later, with a combination of resignation and trepidation, I call the number ...

𝔅eginnings

During World War II (1939-45), my father fights for 6 years as a soldier in Adolf Hitler's *Waffen*-SS.

On the back of this 1944 photo, father writes to his parents, "I know what you are thinking. But I am who I am."

1

On the one hand, he's a non-commissioned officer in a Panzer Division (not a camp guard). On the other hand, for the rest of his life he retains his Nazi-inspired worldview. After the war, father returns to his native South Tyrol (a primarily German-dialect speaking region of northernmost Italy), and through hard work becomes a wealthy and charismatic business owner.

In the summer of 1957, he marries my future mother, a beautiful vivacious woman 16 years his junior. I'm born in September 1958, the only child of their marriage.

After many tempestuous breakups, soon followed by romantic reconciliations, mother leaves us for good (save for a few brief visits), when I'm only 5. Now it's just the 2 of us.

I grow up as father's "SS Princess" in public, with a glamorous wardrobe and expensive trips to luxurious locales. But at home, I'm subjected to almost daily emotional and physical abuse, and often to sexually inappropriate conduct that falls just short of physically molesting me.

To numb my pain, at age 14 I get hooked on heroin with Fabio, my drug-dealing boyfriend. Father dies when I'm 21, and in less than 3 years Fabio and I (by then we have 2 sons) have gone through my inheritance, an estate worth a few million dollars. The last straw is catching Fabio and my cousin Astrid in bed together. (I had looked up to her as a role model since early childhood.) I then leave him for good.

The Downward Spiral

By 1982, I'm living in my car with my sons, Johan and Lukas. Having learned of our condition from others, mother travels to South Tyrol, obtains legal custody of my boys, and takes them to America (where she's been living since leaving father and me). To help me recover from heroin addiction, she lets me live at her home in Easton, Maryland with my sons —and her sexual-predator 3rd husband, Rod.

And so at age 24, having just lost custody of Lukas and Johan, I arrive in America with, as mentioned, about $20 to my name, no green card, an 8th grade education, little fluency in English, and a 1-oz. packet of heroin.

To her eternal credit, mother takes me daily to a methadone clinic in Salisbury, Maryland. The clinic gives me a relatively low dose of methadone, so my withdrawal won't drag on for years (as was happening back in Italy). But meanwhile, because of the low dose, I feel very sick all the time.

For the first 3 months, I get so little sleep it feels as if I'm not getting any at all. One night while I'm still exhausted and vulnerable (after he's arranged for the rest of the family to be away), Rod plies me with liquor — and then rapes me.

Now that I'm off heroin (not for the 1st time in my life), the next issue is staying off for good. Mother's hairdresser, Elise, recommends to her that I join Narcotics Anonymous (NA), a program for recovering addicts based upon the 12 Steps of Alcoholics Anonymous (AA). (For more information about these programs, see www.na.org and www.aa.org.)

Elise puts me in touch with Drew, a very dedicated member of NA. To help still sick and suffering addicts, and to "keep it green" for himself, Drew earnestly works NA's 12th Step: *Having had a spiritual awakening as a result of [Steps 1-11], we tried to carry this message to addicts*. Drew is kind enough to drive for an hour to pick me up in Easton, then an hour to his "home meeting" in Annapolis, and after the meeting drive me back to Easton.

For the most part, I'm able to shut out everything else in my life, and focus on staying clean *and* sober. NA's "1 day at a time" approach greatly helps. The Serenity Prayer — *Lord, grant me the serenity to accept the things I cannot change, courage to change the things I can, and the wisdom to know the difference* — also really helps. I say this prayer a lot during this period. While I'm very unhappy with how my life has turned out so far, I do my best to *accept life on life's terms*, as the program saying goes.

But at first, I have a stiff drink before Drew picks me up. I confide in him I'm drinking to lessen the anxiety I feel from living under the same roof with a step-father who raped me, yet too afraid to say anything that might jeopardize the financial support Rod provides to my mother, my younger sister (via mother's 2nd husband), and my 2 sons.

Drew cautions that I have to get out of that house if I'm ever to get completely clean and dry. He offers to let me live in his place with a few other guys in NA. I'd just have to cook and clean for them — no strings attached. I accept his offer, doing to Johan and Lukas what mother did to me (though I vowed I never would): *leaving them behind.*

I sleep on a pullout couch in the living room. Everyone at Drew's is a caring person so, thankfully, it's a safe space (unlike Rod's home). Though Drew is known to be a wo-manizer, it's obvious that I'm like a lost puppy. So, unlike Rod with his nightly lewd exhibitionism, Drew doesn't try to take advantage of me.

My biggest concern is that I'm not getting to see my sons very often. It's a burden on mother to bring them to Anna-polis which, as noted, is about an hour's drive each way. But, I can sometimes visit them in Easton, when I can get a ride there and back.

A few months later, I get a job shoving pizzas and calzones in and out of the oven at an Italian pizza parlor (my arms are still scarred from oven burns). This enables me to move into an apartment with 2 other women. Each of us pay rent of $50/month.

𝔍ames

I Hate You — Don't Leave Me: Understanding the Borderline Personality, by Jerold Kreisman and Hal Strauss, is a wonderful self-help book. The title sums up the way I've felt about several relationships I've been in.

At the end of my 1ˢᵗ month clean and sober, Drew takes me to the 1982 Narcotics Anonymous Convention in Philadelphia. There I meet Drew's friend James, a New Yorker who's been clean and sober for 2 years.

In September 1983, I see James again, this time at an NA convention in New York City. Soon we're dating. A year later, the job I then have (sales work in a women's clothing chain) reassigns me from Maryland to Manhattan. In September 1984, I move into James's Queens, NY apartment.

Having grown up in a small, slow-moving town in the Alps, I experience culture shock due to NYC's enormous size and hi-speed pace. (I don't even know what Kmart is.) But, I feel safe living with James. Since he's from NYC, he knows how everything works here. For the 1ˢᵗ time since father died, I have someone in my life who's looking out for me.

In February 1985, James and I wed in a civil ceremony in Baltimore. Now that I'm married, mother returns custody of the 2 most precious people in my life: Johan and Lukas.

Marrying James allows me to apply for a green card. But, it isn't a "green-card marriage", in the sense of a sham relationship. Although I'm not head-over-heels in love with James, nonetheless he's good to me, he takes care of a lot of things, and he's very protective. I have great respect for him, and I sincerely want the marriage to work.

However, now that I'm clean and dry, I finally get in touch with my anger at the abuse I endured from father. Regrettably, this anger boils over onto James. Before long, I'm unable to bear his attempts at physical intimacy.

I'm experiencing a form of PTSD (though I don't realize it at the time). For example, if James tries to hold my hand, I pull my hand away from him and, feeling totally enraged, I start a fight!

He'd ask, "What's the matter with you?"

At first, neither of us is aware that when James tries to hold my hand, the anger resurfaces that I felt when father made me hold *his* hand — as if we were a romantic couple. I wasn't allowed to say, *Please don't put your hand on my leg*, when he'd lean over while driving the car, and put his hand on my inner thigh, as if we were lovers. I couldn't say *no* to father about *anything*. I had to smile and reassure him daily with words like, "It's okay, Papi", "No problem", "I love you", etc — concealing my rage.

So, once I'm clean and sober, poor James gets the brunt of all my suppressed anger at father. Within 6 months of our marriage, I have come to *hate* James! Yet, I feel very guilty about it. I know this can't be his fault, because he's treating me very well. And yet, I still can't help feeling this way.

At some point, James realizes what's going on beneath the surface, and says to me, "You need to go into therapy to work through these issues, because *I'm* not your father." So, James is the one who makes me realize I have psychological issues stemming from father's abuse, and I need to address these issues in therapy. For this alone, I will forever be grateful to James.

Still, I can no longer remain married to him. Understandably, he's deeply disappointed when I tell him I have to go.

I find a nearby apartment. (I think Rod, who has been sending me monthly "guilt money" {though it's never described as that} is the one who helps me with the deposit.)

James asks that I move out when he isn't home. So, one summer weekend, when Lukas has just turned 7 and Johan isn't yet 3½, we walk the 3 blocks from one apartment to the other, carrying in our arms what little we own.

Working Hard to be Poor

For the next few years, I continue working for minimum wage, or barely above it, as sales help in women's clothing stores. For 6 days a week, my lunch is a 75¢ potato knish with mustard. I get home exhausted, having little time and energy to be a mother to Lukas and Johan — after having already been away from them for 10 hours. Yet, I hardly have money to feed them, and I have great difficulty finding a responsible babysitter for what I can afford to pay.

In short: We're dirt poor.

Because I'm multilingual, I'm able to find work in a series of upscale women's clothing stores on Manhattan's fashionable Madison Avenue (making a little more money with each move). But, I'm not feeling fashionable myself. As noted, I emigrated to America with an 8th grade education and a heroin/methadone habit. My drug habit is finally behind me (by the grace of God), but I still lack formal schooling, and now I'm a single mother raising my 2 young boys in poverty.

Past years of heroin and methadone addiction, plus poor dental hygiene and eating too much sugary food, have badly damaged my teeth. But, I don't have money for dental care.

All in all, I feel very bad about myself.

Therapy

As James urged me to do, I seek psychotherapy. I get into a group, as well as having individual appointments. The group's members include 3 successful jazz musicians, a very nice older man, and 2 women.

At the time, I don't relate well to women. Because mother left when I was so young, and I was something of a tomboy growing up, I'm clueless about other women, and how to be around them. (Ironically, my only female friend of the time is James's ex-girlfriend.)

𝕵𝖔𝖊 𝕶𝖊𝖜𝖑

In February 1986, I'm still going to NA meetings and group therapy when jazz legend Joe Kewl (accompanied by his entourage) walks into the store I'm working in. Seeing me, he asks the manager that I be the one who assists him.

After making his purchases, he gives me his phone number, and tells me to call him. I give him mine, and tell him he'll have to call me if he wants to talk more. Soon he does call, and after a few conversations, I agree to go on a date with him. Before long, we're dating regularly.

By coincidence, all the jazz musicians in our group have worked with Joe at one time or another. (That 3 men in my group already know a guy I've just started dating feels weird.) They warn me, *Joe is a crazy drug addict. He pops pills. Be careful. You're in recovery and doing well. You might relapse if you date him.*

I wish I'd taken their advice. By dating Joe, I avoid working on my unresolved issues about my parents, and instead continue in the same patterns. Like father, Joe is very emotionally abusive. Oddly, I don't have much problem with that — because that's what I grew up with. However, Joe and I don't live together. If we did, I don't think we'd have kept dating for the 1½ years our relationship lasts.

Once I start dating Joe, I stop going to therapy. As the guys in my group had warned, Joe offers me "black beauties" (ie, amphetamine), Vicodin, and Tylenol with codeine. Because I'm feeling so overwhelmed at the time, I take these drugs when I'm with him.

Joe's being 22 years older than I am is another way that dating him is like being with father again. Although Joe is very different from father in most respects, there's some emotional familiarity in our relationship. As noted, Joe is choleric and abusive like father was — and I'm already used to handling a complicated and difficult man.

Joe does have his nice moments (though they're few and far

between). For now, I live for these nice moments with him.

And, in a way, Joe provides a glimmer of hope that I'll someday escape from poverty. Working in a clothing store for the fashionably wealthy on Madison Avenue may sound a little glamorous. But, the truth is that these jobs are long, stressful, and pay very little — certainly not enough for a single mother to raise 2 sons in NYC.

To be clear, although Joe can be generous now and then, he's not financially supporting me. But, dating him is occasionally like the life I knew growing up with father in Europe. There's some elegance and sophistication when I'm with Joe.

After a year and a half of our on-again/off-again relationship, I catch Joe with another woman, and that ends it for good.

Carlos

After I break up with Joe, I meet Carlos. Like James, Carlos is a good man who is kind to me. Unfortunately, like Joe, Carlos is heavily into drugs, in his case cocaine. Carlos wants to marry me, and looking back, I should have accepted his proposal (once he got clean). But, as with James, I eventually become repelled when he tries to touch me.

I get furious even when Carlos only wants to hug me, or show affection any other way, never mind to have sex. I can not tolerate just being next to him. I feel like a trapped animal struggling to escape a cage, and it's a feeling I hate. And yet, I don't hate *him*. On the contrary, I *love* Carlos. He's been very good to my sons and me. I care about him a lot, and I'd never want anything bad to happen to him. But when I'm lying in bed next to him, even the thought that he might affectionately touch me makes my hair stand on end.

However, as with James, I feel very conflicted. I can't understand why I feel rage toward Carlos, and I feel terrible about it. Still, it gets to the point that I have to end our relationship, just as I had to break up with James. I have Carlos move out, and I feel very relieved afterward.

And yet, doing what is best for me comes at the cost of feeling incredible guilt, because I know Carlos is a good man, and that he truly loves me.

The Harm Doesn't End When the Abuse Ends

It's a powerful truth for a lot of people who've been sexually abused that they later have strong emotional reactions to being touched, even by someone they love.

Though these triggers were formed in the past, for many victims it's impossible in the present to be in a healthy intimate relationship. I come to feel I'm hopeless, that I'll never be able to love someone in a healthy way.

I've already been in Narcotics Anonymous, Alcoholics Anonymous, individual therapy for several years, and group therapy on and off. Later, I go to meetings of Adult Children of Alcoholics, Codependency Anonymous, and eventually Sexual Compulsives Anonymous. I go to these different 12-Step meetings trying my best to get to a place where I can tolerate physical and emotional closeness with my partner.

But, I still can't endure even platonic friendships with men, nor with women. Of course, I meet people in NA, and become acquainted with a few of them. I even form a couple of passing friendships. But, it's difficult for me to maintain even these casual friendships for any length of time.

Early on in NA, I'm unofficially assigned a sponsor. (As mentioned, a program sponsor is someone who's been clean for awhile, and is experienced at working the 12 Steps. The relationship is voluntary.) The sponsor I'm assigned is about my mother's age and, unlike me, her addiction is to prescription medication, not street drugs. I speak with her maybe twice, and find that her life experience is too different for me to relate to. My wounds include abandonment by mother. Because of my unresolved feelings about her, having a 12-Step sponsor mother's age feels too "parental".

In addition to my abandonment issues, I have unresolved emotional wounds from father's having totally dominated me, especially his sexual violations. And so, in my romantic relationships, either I fear a man, or I control him. I can never be in a healthy relationship between equals. It's as if I'm on a seesaw. Either I have more power, or he does.

Summing Up the Men in My Life Til Now

I never recoil from Fabio, the father of our sons. But in the end, I lose respect for his being so irresponsible, and I'm the one who leaves the relationship. The same with James — I end up leaving him. However, in retrospect, I can see that James was a much healthier person than Fabio, who had an abusive father himself, and was very depressed.

And then there is Joe. As a world famous celebrity, he can get away with behavior most of us can't. So, he's allowed to act out his narcissism and grandiosity, and he's very abusive and domineering when he does.

After Joe, there's Carlos. Looking back, I realize that Carlos would have been a good husband. But I react to Carlos as I did to James — I can't tolerate his touch.

When I'm growing up, father never allows me to be assertive, or to speak up for myself at all. As mentioned, when he holds my hand in an inappropriately intimate way, I'm not allowed to withdraw my hand. I have to submit to whatever pleases him, whatever he wants. No girl should have to endure being made to sleep in the same bed with her father until she's 13, and even after that, having to spend long periods with him in his sauna while they're both nude.

Early on in my drug-free life, I go to the other extreme from passive acceptance. When the long-buried rage I felt toward father comes up to the surface, I feel a need to get rid of whichever man is then in my life. And yet, I would miss the very same man once I've left him. These symptoms are typical of "borderline personality", which is the subject of the book I referred to earlier, *I Hate You — Don't Leave Me*.

It's a kind of push-pull: If someone is close to me, I feel I have to push them away. But, after they go, I want them back. It's a very painful dynamic.

Boundaries

I think that when a child is never allowed to be herself, when she has no privacy or space of her own — because it's never about her, it's always about the needs of someone else — the child grows up to be very sensitive to people not allowing her enough space. So, I've always had a big issue with boundaries. If someone is too close to me, I feel my boundaries are being violated.

It's a delicate balance. Naturally, when someone is very nice and does things for me, at one level I appreciate it. And yet, when it makes me feel I'm being played, I start to have a boundaries issue. Someone whose altruism is almost over the top may be seeking (perhaps unconsciously) to manipulate me into rewarding them for their altruism.

So, if I feel someone is being genuine, I will gratefully accept their help. But if I sense someone is inauthentic, I feel I'm being used. It's coming from *their* need to give, not *my* need to receive. In that case, I want to flee.

These are the 2 types of men I would attract — men who couldn't give at all, or ones who give because of their own neediness, or their need to manipulate me. (At least that's how I felt about the 2nd group.)

Plus, starting with father, I've always been someone's care-taker. In a way, that too is a flaw, because I haven't been entirely altruistic. Yes, I do help people, but there's partly a selfish motive. Not always, but sometimes my caregiving is about controlling the other person.

Also, when someone feels inferior in their early life, they often choose a partner who seems even more inferior, so now that someone can shine. Maybe they choose an alco-holic, drug addict, compulsive gambler, or a partner who can never stand on their own feet. Helping that other per-son makes someone feel like the Good One. But, many times, helping someone who isn't standing on their own feet is keeping them dependent and childlike. In other words, the helper is being an enabler.

Eventually, this becomes intolerable for both people. There really are no winners.

The Last Card in the Deck

Forward Motion

As my relationship with Joe is worsening, I re-enter psychotherapy. This time I go with Johan and Lukas to Astoria Health Clinic for family therapy. Other than Medicaid for a short period of time, I have no health insurance, so I have to pay out of pocket.

Not long after, I begin individual therapy with Anna. Because I feel safe discussing my life with her, I finally share with someone the trauma I've experienced. Although I don't feel I'm growing a lot, Anna definitely provides me with moral support. For example, when I finally break up with Joe, she's there for me.

Besides weekly family therapy, I take my sons to swim at the YMCA twice a week. We do this for a couple of years (in spite of the expense).

In 1987, I get my 1st car. Although I'm dating Joe at the time, he's not the one who helps me buy it. Instead, Vinnie, a neighborhood "wiseguy", co-signs my car loan. He knows I'm struggling, and he just wants to help me out. Now that I have wheels, I drive into Manhattan once a week in the morning to see Anna, while my sons are at school.

Les Préludes

Sometime during our relationship, Joe suggests that I become a call girl (intending it as a compliment). Aside from the obvious concerns about health, safety, self-esteem, and social stigma, I seriously doubt I'm attractive enough to be an escort. But, my continuing financial problems are such that Joe's suggestion remains in the back of my mind.

As noted earlier, while I'm living with him, Carlos's employer requires he go into drug rehab — on unpaid leave. Without the help Carlos has been providing, I fall 3 months behind in the rent, and I'm having trouble feeding my sons consistently.

"Cugines"

There's a little Italian restaurant in my neighborhood called Paradiso Pizza. The owner, Raffaelle, treats my sons and me almost like family, generously helping to feed us during the hard times. One day back in 1985, Raffaelle mentions to me that there's a man in the neighborhood, Tomaso, who'd like to be intimate with me — for money. At the time, I'd recently left my 1st husband, James, and as discussed, my sons and I were really poor. I agree to meet Tomaso.

Though he really wasn't that old, at the time Tomaso seemed to me like a repulsive old man. He paid me all of $50. Afterward, I was so disgusted by the whole situation that I cried for the rest of the day.

These days when I see Tomaso around the neighborhood, I still cross the street to avoid him. Although he must be in his 80's by now, I'm afraid I'm going to punch him in the face. The poor devil might die at anytime. But, it was my first-ever paid experience, and it left me feeling horrible.

Same *cugines*, years later.

Of course, I'm still friends with Raffaelle. It wasn't his fault. Many men in the neighborhood pay to play on the sly. They always seem to know someone who's "connected", and owns an adult-massage parlor or an adult-escort service.

Jerry's

In spite of the disgust I felt about my experience with Serioso, by 1987 I'm again desperate to give my sons a better life. And so, one day when I'm struggling to make ends meet (as usual), I decide to give paid intimacy another try. I buy an issue of the *Village Voice* (a now defunct NYC alternative weekly) and dial the number in 1 of the ads offering work for call girls.

Jerry answers the phone of his "outcall" service (ie, the encounter is at the client's place). He says, "Come on over — you can make a couple of hundred dollars right away."

I go to his office. Lots of phone lines crisscross the room (this is before cellphones are in wide use). Jerry's a huge guy with size 13 feet and a tiny dog that barks all the time. I immediately sense that he's a complete wacko. In the midst of this mess, Jerry keeps snorting cocaine — while drinking Scotch.

As promised, he sends me on a call right away, to a fancy apartment on the Upper West Side of Manhattan. Like Jerry, the client has already been doing lots of cocaine.

The client wants me to lie on his bed and pretend I'm sleeping. He'll act like he's come in through the window and then "pretend" to rape me. (It's his idea of having a good time!)

I'm totally freaked out — unable to handle this situation at all. So, I leave and return to Jerry's office. Right away, he sends me on another call.

The 2nd client is drinking whiskey straight from the bottle, and is already really drunk when I arrive. I'm completely freaked out again. Realizing this, he says to me, "You're not the girl I'm looking for. I don't care about the money — I'll pay you anyway. Go back to your agency and tell Jerry to send me someone else."

I'm really relieved to get out of there. I go back to Jerry's little room. He sends me out on 2 more calls that night. Both of them are doing cocaine and drinking. In the 1980's, lots of people with too much money use cocaine. Many delude themselves that cocaine isn't addictive, thinking they're superior to heroin addicts. They act out sexually all over the place. Yet when they can't reach climax, they go crazy and stay awake all night.

So this is Jerry's client base — crazy drunken coke addicts, like himself. At the end of the evening I say, "Jerry, I can't do this." I work for him only that 1 night. I think, *This is insane. I'll never do this again.*

Two Different Worlds

A year earlier, I left retail clothing sales, and started a job as a residential rental agent in suburban Queens. This does not work out well either, because the pay is commission-only. As a single mom, I'm trying desperately to find work that gives me enough time with my children. But also, work that pays enough to cover my bills.

Now that I'm a rental agent, every day I see really luxurious apartments that rent for $5,000 to $20,000 a month. These suites are located on the Upper Eastside and Westside of Manhattan, and are manned 24/7 by doormen in spiffy uniforms. For example, I might show a duplex penthouse with a 360° wraparound terrace, swimming pool, and floor-to-ceiling windows. It's disheartening that people living in such luxury have so much, while my sons and I are so poor. We're not homeless (so far), but I have to constantly worry about paying just for cheap food and my modest rent.

Working in real estate brings me face to face with NYC's extreme income inequality. There are many homeless people who own nothing but the clothes they're wearing and what they can carry in 1 or 2 shopping bags. Homelessness was particularly severe in NYC in the 1980's (and it's getting worse again). Yet, there are some New Yorkers with private helicopters! Such different worlds. Such extremes.

Background: Luxury apartments along Central Park West.

I didn't see this when I was growing up in Europe. Admittedly, father and I were materially privileged. In my youth, I never worried about money. I shopped for whatever I wanted-ed, and father paid my bills at the end of the month. We had our own home, with a big backyard, a large swimming pool, an abundant fruit orchard, 2 expensive cars, and a vacation home in the mountains. When traveling, we stayed in 5-star hotels and dined in fine restaurants.

On a single shopping trip, it was typical of his unfailing generosity (with everyone, friend or foe) for father to buy me several beautiful dresses, or some fine leather handbags, or a few pairs of Italian handmade shoes.

Yet, though few townspeople had as much as we did, most of the kids in my school were middle-class or even upper-middle-class. To be sure, some people weren't quite middle class, but they were doing okay. In sum, unlike NYC, no one was extravagantly wealthy, or desperately poor.

Homeless in NYC.

Dark Karma

From the start, the price tag for my material good fortune was enduring father's physical and emotional abuse. As noted, I took up heroin at age 14 to numb the pain his abuse made me feel. After father died, he left me an estate so valuable that I would never have had to work again.

However, there was dark karma surrounding the whole thing. Father had been in the military branch of the SS as a non-commissioned officer doing tank repair (not that different from the tractor business he started after the war). But, being in the SS was a crime in itself. Yet, he evaded imprisonment after the war (details in Book I). Even his brother, my Uncle Hubert (who was as kind and gentle as any man I've ever known), served some prison time for having been in the military SS. Perhaps it was because of this bad karma that in the end I lost to heroin everything I'd inherited from father.

Admittedly, when I traveled with Joe Kewl, I got to briefly revisit the lifestyle I had while growing up. For example, we flew 1st class to Rome, Marseille, and Montreux, staying in 5-star hotels wherever we went — just like when I traveled with father. And yet, with Joe too, there was much of the same dark karma.

Now that I'm living in NYC as a single mom, all the material luxuries I had once taken for granted are gone. I'm desperate. I have 2 small sons, little formal education, and no reliable man in my life. At this point (the late 1980's), I don't know what to do. I have no idea what else I *can* do with an 8th grade education. But, based upon what I'm seeing daily as a real estate agent, and what I've experienced while traveling with Joe, I tell myself, *There has to be a better way.*

Seeing what's out there for others gives me a little bit more courage. I vow to myself, *I'm going to fight for something!* (Even though I'm not sure *what.*)

Cara Mia

**Cara mia, why ...
must we say goodbye?**
(Lee Lange and Tulio Trapani)

I wrote in Book I:

> Astrid [my favorite cousin] is diagnosed as bipolar at
> age 18. She attempts suicide several times before she is
> 30. Because of a personal tragedy…at age 37 she jumps
> off the balcony of her 6th story apartment. She survives,
> but her ankles and feet are broken, and her hips are
> shattered. Some of her internal organs are severely in-
> jured, and she spends the rest of her life severely dis-
> abled — emotionally and physically — living in mental
> hospitals and group homes. After many operations, she
> dies in September 2008, at age 52. As mentioned,
> Astrid was like an older sister to me — the one truly
> empathetic witness to the daily terror I endured while
> living with father. Perhaps in some way she too was
> abused by father — I will never know for sure. As if
> there were not enough ironies already, Astrid and father
> are buried in the same grave in a little church cemetery
> in Bolzitano [my hometown in South Tyrol].

What I leave out of this account is why Astrid attempts to
kill herself in 1993. I ended my relationship with Fabio, the
father of my sons, after catching him in an affair with
Astrid(!) Fabio doesn't marry Astrid either (marriage isn't a
part of Fabio's life plan), but they have a baby girl, Cara.
Because Fabio has no visible means of support, and Astrid
already has a long history of psychological issues, the child
welfare authorities in Italy take Cara away from her, and
put Cara up for adoption.

(I offered to raise Cara myself. By then, as will be explained,
I'm financially in a position to do so. But I too am single, so
the authorities nix that idea.)

Her grief over losing Cara causes Astrid to attempt suicide.
Cara's adoption is anonymous for both sets of parents, as is

typical. But, Italy now allows adult adoptees to learn the identity of their biological parents if genetics-based medical concerns are present. Cara's adoption records fall under this category, because of Astrid's mental health history.

Sometime in early 2014, Cara, now that she's 21, uses this law to learn that Astrid and Fabio are her biological parents. In August 2014, Cara contacts my family in Bolzitano for the 1st time. That's when Cara learns that her mother, by then deceased for 6 years, had attempted suicide because of losing her. My family over there contacts me about this development, and I'm soon in touch with Cara myself.

That fall, I meet up in Munich with another cousin, and we travel together to Bolzitano, where I will celebrate my 56th birthday. Along the way, we trek on foot across the Alps (as mother's paternal grandfather and the rest of her family had done, to seek refuge from war-torn Germany soon after World War II).

Cara and I meet in Bolzitano.

By pre-arrangement, I meet Cara when my cousin and I arrive in Bolzitano. She's the most wonderful young person, endowed with talent, personality, and good looks (she resembles Fabio a lot). In spite of being in pain from early onset arthritis, she also is a women's champion of tamburello, a tennis-like sport popular in Europe.

We all quickly become close. Soon, plans are being made for Cara to visit my sons and me in New York. She has written to Fabio, and they are going to meet the following summer.

But, 9 months after she comes back into our lives, Cara is killed in a head-on auto collision while driving across the Alps. My sons, who are her half-brothers through Fabio, had gotten to know her via Facebook. All of us are devastated by this loss.

Some of us have brief but eventful life journeys. Though eventful in a positive way, Cara's journey was all too brief.

The Third Man

**I'm going to live through this, and when it's over,
I'm never going to be hungry again. No, nor any of my folks
... as God is my witness, I'm never going to be hungry again."**
(Margaret Mitchell, *Gone With the Wind*)

As related in Prologue II, in December 1989 my friend Devorah takes me grocery shopping, and spends $100 on food for me and my sons (a full shopping cart back then). This makes me feel like it's Thanksgiving, Christmas, and Easter combined. Devorah reveals to me that she's gotten the money by doing sex work. She makes it sound so easy that I decide to give it one more try.

My inability to remain in a normal romantic relationship is a large part of my calculation in becoming an escort. I'll make my inability to form a healthy attachment work *for* me, rather than beating myself up over what I can't help.

Ironically, I'm undoing years of childhood abuse followed by drug addiction in *reverse order* to the usual progression: 1st I get off drugs; then I go into therapy; and finally, in early 1989, I get my GED. Only *then* do I become a sex worker.

When Devorah tells me how she made the money to buy so much food for me and my boys, I ask her if I can get a job where she's working. She hesitates, then gives me the number of a different place — an outcall service a woman runs out of her home in Bayside, Queens. When I phone this woman, she tells me she doesn't need another girl right now, but she refers me to a woman in Manhattan who has an adult-massage parlor.

This massage parlor has only 2 girls at a time, and they see only 2 or 3 clients per shift. To my pleasant surprise, all the clients are *sane* (unlike Jerry's), and working there seems like a gift from heaven! By seeing only 2 or 3 clients a day, just 2 or 3 days a week, I'm able to pay the 3 months of rent I owe, and even buy a few Christmas presents and spend holiday time with my sons. It's like I finally can breathe. I ask myself, *How bad can this be?*

𝔐agda's: 𝔏earning 𝔚hile 𝔈arning

**In the depths of winter, I finally learned that within me
there lay an invincible summer.** (Albert Camus, *Summer in Algiers*)

Usually this Manhattan madame keeps girls for only 1 week, because her clients want variety. But, she keeps me an extra week, and then refers me to Magda, another Manhattan massage parlor owner. Magda has a more up-scale clientele. Accordingly, her girls work for her long term.

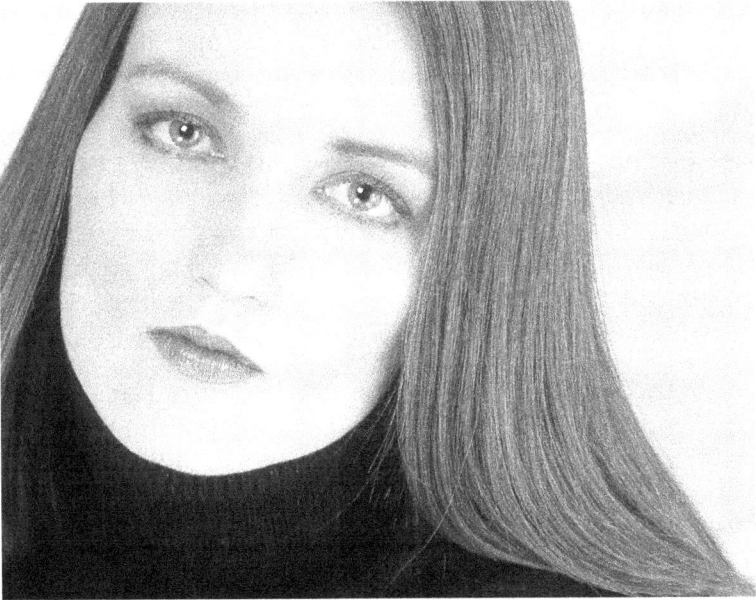

A year or so before I started work at Magda's

During our interview, Magda is warm but professional. She is probably in her mid-40's. Her small massage parlor is located near the corner of 2nd Avenue and East 38th Street, not that far from busy Grand Central Station.

Right away, I feel comfortable with Magda. Everyone's safety, the girls and clients alike, is extremely important to her. Being very cautious, she runs the business like a private club. Her regular clients have been coming there for a number of years. The only new clients she accepts are referrals from existing or former clients. All clients have to know a password to gain admittance to the building.

Magda has a strict dress code. We must wear a white uniform that comes down to our knees, regular pantyhose (no fishnet stockings or crazy patterns), and no weird fingernail polish. A small heel that looks feminine and professional is okay, but not heels that are sky-high or shoes that are vampish. In general, we have to be properly groomed, not wear too much makeup, and look healthy overall.

There are only 2 or 3 girls working at any given time. The day shift is from 10 AM to 6 PM, and the evening shift is from 3 PM to 10 PM. I choose day shifts. I'll be seeing from 1 to 4 clients per shift. A typical session is an hour, during which the client receives a regular massage for most of the time. I'm also expected to make conversation if the client wants that too.

I must not only look professional, I must conduct myself as such. I'm never to solicit any extra money — there's a set price, with no bargaining. In fact, I'm not to discuss money at all. Magda handles all of that before the session. The base fee will be split 50-50 between Magda and me. As is usual in a service business, I get to keep any tips.

Magda runs an impeccable business. Most of her clients are professionals (because it's an expensive pastime). A couple of them *are* a little weird. But they're all safe and sane!

As noted, I've always felt I don't have an attractive face or body. I think I'm fat and my breasts are too small, so I feel unsure of myself when I start at Magda's. But, I also feel genuinely welcome there, so I soon become more comfortable, in spite of my poor body-image.

Hope and Change

From the outset, working at Magda's feels like I've won the lottery! Being there 3 shifts a week leaves 4 whole days for me to be at home with my sons. Finally I have a job that gives me *hope*. For the 1st time in my life, I feel I'm accomplishing something constructive — instead of messing things up left and right. Ironically, sex work gives me my 1st sense of pride. Now that I'm properly caring for myself and my boys on my own, I'm *gaining* self-esteem.

Of course, I can't tell other people what I'm doing, because of the stigma. Hence, I decide to not be in a relationship, or even to date, because I'm not the kind of person who could easily lie to my lover. If a man were to ask me, it'd be really hard to just pretend I'm being faithful to him. On the other hand, it'd be unrealistic to expect a lover to accept my being in this business. I decide not to date, but instead to focus on my schooling.

So, sex work turns out to be not only a great relief financially. It's also psychologically liberating, by having removed romance as an issue in my life. I no longer worry about mistreating a boyfriend — because I don't have one. The pressure of meeting a man who soon wants to get close — and my not being able to handle it — is gone. The constant push-pull, pushing them away but then pulling them back, and doing this over and over, has ended. It was so exhausting, and it created such guilt. I've felt like I'm a terrible person for having treated so badly guys who have been so good to me.

Learning to Laugh Again

During this period, I do make one new male friend, Giorgio. Our relationship is platonic, which works fine for both of us, as he's married with family. Giorgio visits us once in a while. He's always in a good mood, and teaches me to not be so serious, to smile and laugh again. He reminds me that a sense of humor is really important.

I had forgotten I even have a sense of humor, and that it's okay to laugh at my crazy life. It's been over 20 years since I've been able to really laugh. After mother leaves, I live under father's loving yet abusive domination in the years that follow, so I really don't have much to laugh about. Once I'm in America, I begin recovering from heroin addiction — but with no sense of self-worth. I'm a broken spirit, and I kind of harden. I'm in survival mode almost all of the time, so I don't get to do much that is fun. That whole part of me shuts down.

Then Giorgio comes into my life and lifts my spirit. From the moment we meet, Giorgio is lots of fun to be with. Like me, he has 2 boys. We'd take them all skateboarding and rollerblading in Central Park. For the 1st time in many years, I'm laughing and having fun.

Giorgio would say things like, "You don't need to go to NA and AA meetings, listening to people go on and on about the drugs and alcohol in their past, and their sadness and suffering now. All you need is to go to a comedy show and have some fun!"

Of course, this is a considerable exaggeration. NA and AA have been crucial in saving my life. But, Giorgio helps me connect to the lost part of me that is playful. I meet his wife. Though they are officially separated, they are back and forth together. We all become good friends.

Aside from Giorgio, his family, and my sons, there are no other people in my social life during this period.

Working My Way Through School

The sex business is a big relief in another important way. I'm able to focus on school, which, along with raising my boys, has become my main goal in life. I realize that I need to get more education if I don't want the 3 of us to wind up in a homeless shelter. In 1989, having gotten my GED earlier in the year, I decide to go to university so I can have a real profession. I will use any means necessary to accomplish this, as long as I'm not hurting myself or others.

Working for Magda is what makes it possible for me to go to college. As noted, I start at Magda's near the beginning of 1990. By the fall of 1990, I'm enrolled in Kingston College, one of the more selective colleges in NYC. I read my schoolbooks when I'm between massage sessions. At Magda's, the girls aren't there because this is their dream career. They're there because they have children to support, or they're going to school, or trying to better themselves some other way.

𝕸agda's 𝕲irls

I think that having done sex work has made me a better person — and a more perceptive therapist. I not only understand *men* better. By interacting with other adult-companions, I've learned a lot about *women* I didn't know before (because I grew up without a mother to teach me).

Before doing this work, I hadn't experienced sisterhood. For example, how a woman deals with being "picked", how she's treated by the others, and how they deal with *not* being picked. Most of all, how women support each other by saying things like, *If you didn't make much money this shift, don't worry, you'll make more on the next — it always averages out. One night you make more money; one night you make less. You needn't take it personally.* And, women would give each other compliments like, *You're so beautiful!*

There's also the joking. It can be hard sitting there just waiting. Admittedly, there are times I would feel low because my life has turned out this way. (Even nowadays, though I've become successful by socially accepted standards, I still feel this way sometimes.) But, then a girl would make a joke, and I'd crack up laughing — seeing the lightness of things, and not taking myself too seriously.

For instance, at times I could fall into a whole mindset like, *Look what I'm doing! Look where I am! Look where life has taken me! I'm working in a brothel — is this really a life?* But then there would be a girl who says, "This is just what we do for money. We have our life outside of here, with our children and other family, plus our hopes and dreams.

"It's like being a waitress when a customer slaps you on the ass. You have to put up with that, but it's just a job." (This feeling of *don't feel down — it's just a job* hasn't been a shared experience for me in previous work environments.)

With adult-companionship, at least you know the deal. It's more honest in that way. There's an exchange. Both sides of the exchange get what they bargain for. So, it's win-win (unlike so much else in life).

Meow

At times, though, a girl could be very catty. If one girl is getting a lot more clients than average, another girl might make a barbed comment like, *"I* probably should do it without a condom too." Or, "Be careful — she does *everything."*

Unfortunately, some guys see a girl over and over because she's allowing them to have unsafe sex. But most men, especially if they're married (which the great majority of clients are), don't want unsafe sex. They worry about contracting an STD — and bringing it home to their wife.

On the other hand, although many men seek variety, some escort/client pairings "click". And so, he becomes a "regular". Sometimes such pairings become long-term platonic friendships. (I still have several such friends myself.) However, if a girl has lots of regulars right away, other girls naturally become suspicious. So, there'd be gossip about girls who were making much more money than the rest of us.

But for the most part, we stick together. I had so much fun with the girls I worked with that I'm sorry I haven't kept in touch with more of them. We've had a good many shared experiences that only we really understand.

Of course, I've had interesting experiences with clients too. After all, many of these men are successful, and in a few cases famous. (Some of the ones who are famous for their creative endeavors are surprisingly uncreative in private.)

Yet, I feel sorry for the women who are almost 50, haven't saved much money, and don't have a career alternative. They're stuck, and it's pretty sad.

For me, the business is a means of getting the formal education I didn't get earlier. I reassure myself that it's a temporary detour while I get my life back on track.

Unforgettable Women

Reba is petite with beautiful long hair and a sweet bubbly personality. She has a son and, like me, works at Magda's just 3 or 4 days a week. She's been there several years, and has a roster of regular clients. Reba gives me a "heads up" on what to expect from clients.

Margot

Reba's friend Margot has a build that is very different from Reba's. Margot is tall (about 5' 9"), with short blonde hair. Like me, she has an athletic build, though she's bigger than I am. Yet she seems to have pretty good self-esteem, plus a nice open personality, and no problem accepting her looks as they are. That Margot feels good about her body helps me feel good about *my* body. It shows me that it's okay to not be petite, and to not have Pamela Anderson curves.

Tanya

Tanya is older but still very pretty, with long black hair and an enhanced bustline. She's very nice too and, like Margot, she's acquired many regular clients over time.

Angela

Angela, in my view, has the hottest body of us all. She's a year older than I am, which makes her 32 when we meet. Angela is petite with small breasts, but she's muscular and toned. She regularly works out at a gym, and her behind is so firm you could stand a quarter on it. She's built — and she knows it. She struts about showing off her body and, unsurprisingly, she's very much in demand by clients.

Angela's husband knows she works at Magda's. He drops her off there, and picks her up when her shift is over. They are investing money in real estate, and have a home in New Jersey, as well as several buildings in Brooklyn.

They're also into swinging at sex clubs. This is all new to me. I've certainly had sexual experiences with different men, but I'm still naive about sex beyond the ordinary. I don't think I've ever worn a thong at this point. As a hippie-type, I have hardly even worn a *bra*.

Angela isn't always the nicest girl. She does have her favorites, but there's always a girl she can't stand. That girl becomes a villain in Angela's eyes.

For example, she doesn't like Margot. I think Angela has a problem with big-boned girls, or chubby girls who don't work out and aren't toned. I'm always a little intimidated by Angela, because although I'm not really fat, in my eyes I'm at least 10 to 15 pounds heavier than I should be.

For some reason, I want Angela to like me, so I seek her approval. I must say, she teaches me a lot. For example, she advises me to give a strong massage initially, but then to become softer and more sensual. The straight massage part lasts for at least 30 to 40 minutes (stretching out this part as long as possible). The actual sex is maybe 10 minutes, or even less, making it the shortest part of the session.

Sometimes a client asks for a "double", meaning he wants 2 girls. I learn from Angela to handle these requests in a sophisticated way. Of course, I'm happy for the girls who feel real passion for each other. But, even though it's not my thing, Angela shows me how to pretend it is. The men don't seem to know the difference. It's funny how excited they get, thinking they're the hottest stud on the planet. So, I do learn a lot from Angela.

Angela's Marriage

I'm ambivalent about Angela's unusual marriage. I wonder whether I should envy her for having a great relationship with a man who knows everything that's going on? I ask her, "How can your husband accept your being in this business? How can he not be jealous?"

She answers, "Because I never climax at work. What I do here is just a job — making men feel sexy and good about themselves. Then I go home and really make love with my husband. For me, it's no different from being a waitress, secretary, nurse, or any other service worker."

Self-Esteem

I come to realize that Angela has a point — in the end it's just a job. For the most part, I don't feel what I'm doing is demeaning or humiliating. As mentioned, it actually is the 1st job in my life that *raises* my sense of self-esteem. I'm bringing home enough money to pay my bills, but still have enough time and energy left over to be a parent who's there for my sons.

Plus, there's some money left over for things like taking them to Great Adventure in the summer. Or, giving them a birthday party, or buying them a gift or treat. Something special once in a while. (These are things we hadn't been able to do — unless I was living with a man whose touch I dreaded.)

To be sure, the boys and I don't go to 5-star hotels (like the places father took me to). But we sometimes go away to the country for a weekend, or to the beach. Normal stuff. The kinds of things any parent wants for their children.

So now, I don't feel like a loser after working on my feet 10 hours straight in a retail shop, and then getting home with my legs hurting like hell, and yet still unable to provide enough food for my sons.

I'm no longer working on Saturdays and Sundays, with my older son, Lukas, watching his 4-year's younger brother, Johan, because I can't afford a weekend babysitter. Lukas no longer has to call me while I'm working in Manhattan to tell me Johan has fallen and is bleeding. And then exclaim, "What should I do, Mom? I don't know what to do!"

I couldn't go home from my jobs in retail to deal with a family emergency, as would arise from time to time, because if I left early, or even if I took a sick day, I'd be fired. (By contrast, Magda is much more understanding about such matters.) When I was working in retail, I'd have to stay in the store listening to one of my sons crying over the phone, while I was stuck doing a meaningless job. (How important is it to "accessorize"?) A job that didn't pay enough for me to make ends meet.

All of those feelings of failure, financial anxiety, and inadequacy as a mother are gone now that I'm working for Magda. So, this work really does lift my sense of self-worth.

The Secret Life of Men

I don't remember what I thought, before I became an escort, about men who pay for adult-companionship. Maybe I felt that they are scary guys who want to hurt women, or just creepy in general, since that's how they're typically portrayed in the media. (That night I worked for Jerry couldn't have improved my view of them.)

But, once I'm in the business at a safe and sane establishment, I learn that most clients are just average guys with an above-average income. Since it's an expensive pastime, many are lawyers, doctors, or in finance, along with well-paid union workers in both the public and private sectors.

Besides higher income, the personal qualities of Magda's clients is a pleasant surprise. They're all respectful! There's no craziness. No one brings in alcohol or drugs, or arrives drunk or high on drugs. The clients typically come in at lunchtime, or right after work. The vast majority are married men who love their wife and children, and have no intention of leaving them. But, they're missing something in their home life, so they seek out an adult-companion.

It's comfortable. I'm treated like a friend. They usually come weekly, or once or twice a month. We make conversation, and I get to know them. I learn their wife's name, their children's names, and what's new in their personal life. After getting word from Magda, I might feel, *Rick from Boston is coming. That's great — I haven't seen him in awhile!*

Naturally, there are creeps in any pool of men. But for the most part, my clients are lovely guys who treat me better than my loser/cheater boyfriends have treated me. Some clients bring presents — sentimental things like cologne, lingerie, chocolates. For instance there's the client we call Candy Man, who brings a whole bag of candies, apples, and other fruits, because he wants all the girls to have nice snacks (more about him below).

The education I get about these men is really eye-opening.

Little Brooksie

Brooksie, as he likes to be called, is a short, chubby man in his late 60's. He's a bit eccentric. For instance, he stuffs lots of cash in his pants pockets. Yet otherwise, he always dresses impeccably in an expensive suit with a nice shirt.

In everyday life, he's a wealthy businessman. But when he's at Magda's, he roleplays the part of a nerdy and naive college freshman.

Brooksie would become visibly excited as he'd tell us about the fantasy that he's apparently been thinking about well before arriving at Magda's. He'd request 2 or 3 girls together in a room, giving each girl a different part to play. One might be a dorm proctor, another a college nurse, and the 3rd a professor.

In a typical scenario, Brooksie is lying on a lounge chair by the college's swimming pool. It's a hot summer day, but there's a pleasant breeze. He announces, "Okay, today Heide is my dorm mom, and she's with me at the pool."

(My name at Magda's is "Heide". Magda assigns it to me because, given the demographic makeup of much of her client base, she doesn't want it known that I'm of German ancestry. So, she tells everyone that I'm "Heide from Switzerland". I'm not happy about this, but as the 12-Step saying goes, *acceptance is the key*.)

Still smiling, Brooksie would continue, "Angela, you're a professor. Margot, you're my academic advisor, who comes to check on me." He'd come up with a whole scene in which I'd say something like, "Brooksie, I have very good news for you. Professor Angela is coming by, and she wants to give you a *special* lesson today!"

He'd get all happy and exclaim, "Oh, that's *wonderful!* Where's Professor Angela?" Angela would come to his side and start the "lesson". Of course, the lesson would be Brooksie getting a massage. All of us massage him — one of us takes his right arm; another takes his left arm; a 3rd massages his back.

As his lesson begins, he's still in his underwear. We remove it while we're massaging him. Once he's completely undressed, he babbles, "All these *women!* I don't know what to do! I don't know what's happening to me! A dorm proctor and a professor are both watching! Oh, this is so exciting!"

Then one of us whispers in his ear, "Brooksie, that very nosy academic advisor, Margot, has just arrived. She wants to know what lesson you're getting today. Your other teachers have heard about these lessons you're getting, and they're curious. There may be even *more* teachers coming.

Brooksie then might say, "Oh my, I don't know if I can take that. I'm very embarrassed. I don't know, I'm so *excited*, but I'm also *afraid*. What should I do?"

(It's all so ridiculous, but there's a certain sweetness to it. Yet at the same time, we often feel, *Do we really have to do this again. Here we go, Brooksie, how excited can you get?*)

He continues, "Oh, professor, this is such a great lesson. I don't know what to do, professor."

"Brooksie, just relax and enjoy the lesson."

Eventually he'd climax. He'd then thank each of us individually: "Thank you, Professor Angela. Thank you, Margot. Thank you, Heide. That was such a wonderful lesson!" (He'd then tip us generously.)

More than once a week, we'd put on this show for Brooksie. Magda would say, "Brooksie is coming", and we'd think, *Here we go again!*

But, on a slow day we'd be happy to see Brooksie, because he's such an easy client. We joke and laugh and wink at each other while he's on his stomach. It's the kind of humor that you only experience in this type of setting — when all of us girls are in the same situation.

It's never mean-spirited though. We might chuckle and say, "Oh my God, can you believe this guy visits 2 or 3 times a week — and no one in his family knows. He's a successful business executive in the everyday world, but when he comes here, he acts like he's a clueless college kid!"

I view working at Magda's as partly an opportunity to learn about different types of men. To compare how they behave normally, versus how they behave in places such as Magda's. Ways of being that are completely different. I get insights at Magda's that I don't get anywhere else — certainly not from attaining the BA and MSW degrees in psychology that I eventually earn.

Owen: The Ties That Bind

Owen is another regular at Magda's. He's quite wealthy — his apartment is an entire floor of a famous Upper Westside building that overlooks Central Park. I visit him there once, while his wife and children are on vacation. He gives me the grand tour of his place.

Owen always wears expensive clothing, including suspenders and fine leather shoes. But he especially fancies novelty ties, and has a whole closet full of them. For Christmas, he has a Santa Claus tie. If a button is pressed, the tie sings "Jingle Bells", or "Rudolph the Red-Nosed Reindeer". He also has Mickey Mouse ties, and for St. Valentine's Day, he has ties with hearts. There's a tie for every occasion — hundreds of them in all.

Nathan: Not Too Hot to Handle

I have strong hands, so I give a good straight massage. Nathan likes this, and he becomes a regular. Again, it's a 30- or 40-minute massage, 10 minutes or so of sensual stuff, and then bringing a hot towel and talking with him for the remaining time.

It can't be overemphasized that I'm able to handle this job emotionally *better* than any previous job. I can deal with those 10 minutes, 3 times a day, 3 days a week. It's not such a bad deal. In previous jobs, I'd be on the go all day, not make enough money even to buy a proper lunch for myself — or breakfast and dinner for my sons — and yet get home too exhausted to spend time with them. Too exhausted pretty much for *anything*.

By contrast, working for Magda is emotionally, as well as

financially, rewarding. I become friends with my coworkers, unlike in my previous jobs, and we all have fun while waiting for another client to arrive.

For example there's Martie. She's in her 40's, health-conscious, and wise. She does yoga, meditates, and is into Buddhism. While in the waiting room, she usually sits and knits, or reads a book. It's soothing to be around her. All in all, the girls' waiting area is a very comfortable place to be. (I never had this feeling at other jobs.)

Tim the Lawyer

Tim is a lawyer who, back in the day, loved coming to Magda's to visit me. Tim is another father figure. He was already in his early 60's then. Now he must be in his 80's. (But I think he's still getting sensual massages somewhere.)

He likes to tell the same story about another place that Magda had. There was a fire, and Tim saved everybody by helping them out onto the window ledge. There they waited until fire fighters came. (He'd tell this story over and over.)

He knows people in high places. Though he's a Republican, and a friend of the Bush family, he's also friends with highly placed Democrats. For example, one of his wives (he's been married 3 times) was the commissioner of a well-known NYC government agency.

Tim is a really nice guy. Though I left the business years ago, we've remained friends. For example, at Christmastime, we have lunch at the University Club on 5th Avenue in Manhattan.

He continues to take legal cases, and he's helped me with a few legal matters over the years. (Two of them will be discussed below.) He remains my family lawyer to this day.

Luigi's Garden

Then there's Luigi, another interesting character. He takes the train to Magda's from Princeton Junction, New Jersey all the way into Manhattan (a more than 2-hour ride).

Luigi is probably in his 80's when I meet him(!) He was seeing Magda herself for many years, until she retired from giving massages to just running her business. Luigi often fondly reminisces about Magda. After her, he saw Angela for a long time. Now he frequently talks about her, and how he still loves her very much. (Readers might be surprised to learn how emotionally attached many of the men become.)

Luigi has a vegetable garden in the backyard of his home in suburban New Jersey. During the summer months, he carries a big basket of fresh vegetables all the way from Princeton Junction. Upon arrival at Magda's, Luigi would exclaim, "Ladies, let's have a picnic!"

He'd then set up the room with a tablecloth and napkins. There'd be fresh tomatoes from his garden, along with cheese and crackers he picked up on his way over. So part of his session is pretending we're lovers enjoying a nice picnic on a Sunday afternoon. (Such moments are priceless.)

Luigi is a devoted amateur photographer, and always brings an old-fashioned camera with him. He's fascinated by trains and goes to train museums to photograph them. As a young boy, he sometimes rode with his father on the train to NYC. He has warm memories of arriving at Grand Central Station, and this iconic train terminal continues to be one of the subjects he most enjoys photographing.

On one occasion he says, "I want to photograph you, because someday I won't be able to visit anymore, and it'd be so nice to have a picture to remember you by."

I allow him to take a picture of me — but only with my clothes on. From time to time, Luigi would say something like, "Marlena, it's so wonderful to be with you. You have no idea how happy you make me. When I'm no longer able to visit here, I will sometimes sit in my basement looking at my photographs, remembering you, Angela, and Magda — and the great times I've had."

One day, his son calls to say Luigi has suffered a stroke, and he asked his son to notify me. He recovers after a few months, and resumes having "picnics". Eventually, though, I stop working there and lose contact with Luigi.

Grand Central Station, NYC.

The Candy Man

Candy Man, as we call him, is a lawyer about 40 years old who has never married. He always comes to Magda's with a big bag of candy — M&M's, Hershey's Kisses, and other chocolates and sweets. He's just the nicest guy, but he's unable to romantically connect with a woman in the conventional way, because he's not the most handsome guy, he's overweight, and he's kind of clumsy. Yet, we embrace him because he's very loving and very emotionally giving. He comes to a brothel with a bag full of fruits and candy just to make everyone's day brighter. He'd exclaim, "This is to sweeten up your day!"

Wrestlemania

One client, an older man who is a little weird, always wants to wrestle. He likes to begin wrestling with me while we're both standing. It's kind of ridiculous. I think, *Are you serious? You want me to wrestle with you and then jump on top of you?* But this is what excites him.

(Then there are cross-dressers — men who enjoy wearing exaggeratedly feminine clothing. More on them below.)

Joey the Worm

As clients go, Chasidic Jews (sometimes called "ultra-Orthodox") are due special mention for several reasons: The men choose to call attention to themselves by their distinctive clothing and hair style; they tend to live and work apart from both Gentiles and other Jews; they claim to be more authentically Jewish than other Jews; and though Jews in general are among the most generous and considerate of clients, somebody has to buck the trend.

Lexington Avenue, NYC.

Those who would impose standards of conduct on others — for example, judges, clergymen, police, Scout leaders, politicians, etc. — invite closer scrutiny of their own behavior. I fully realize that some members of the other groups just mentioned also visit me at Magda's. But, the Chasids are the only ones who advertise their group affiliation by the garments they wear on arrival.

There's one Chasid we call "Joey the Worm", because he squirms like a worm while begging to be beaten and insulted. Because of my German accent, he wants *me* to see him, pretending I'm a Nazi while beating him with my shoe, and telling him I'm going to throw him into an oven! We all have our own unresolved trauma, but this is too bizarre and unsettling for me, and I refuse to do it.

Joey works in one of those electronic stores, near Grand Central Station, which cater to tourists, and seem to often have "going out of business" sales. (Savvy New Yorkers go to more established places, like the Chasidic owned and operated B&H Photo Video or Adorama, both of which have the highest ethical standards.)

B&H Photo Video, 9th Avenue, NYC.

The tourist-oriented stores sell everything in the way of consumer electronics, from cameras to computers to stereos and recorded music. Joey would say, "Come to my store and I'll give you a discount." I would think, *I prefer not to.*

One time Joey tells Margot that he wants to pour gasoline over her and set her on fire! After that, she refuses to see him, and he's banned from seeing any of the girls for a time. However, he whines to Magda that he didn't really mean it. He just said a dumb thing. But he'd never actually harm anyone. So, Magda eventually lets him come back (though Margot still won't have a session with him).

Joey likes to go to Le Trapeze, a club for swingers that, as of this writing, is still located on East 27th Street in Manhattan. Joey would hire a girl for the evening, take her with him to Le Trapeze, and then spend his time walking around naked, watching people having sex in a big room. Le Trapeze also has small rooms where couples can either be by themselves, or with another couple if they want.

My one visit to Le Trapeze with Joey is awkward, to put it mildly, because it's a semi-public gathering, and I'm with someone who, because of his attire, obviously isn't my husband or lover. So, everyone there *knows* that I must be a paid escort. And the *hypocrisy* of it all: He's sooo religious — but here he is at a swingers club!

"Follow the Chasids"

Some Chasids spy on each other to learn who among them is visiting Magda's. At times, Magda would say, "Hey, Joey's sitting outside in his car, watching the place."

I don't know if they are blackmailing each other, or what is going on. But, there's a saying in New York: If you want to find a brothel, just follow the Chasids.

One Chasid I meet is a real *sweetheart*. He likes to talk about his 8 children — he's just the nicest guy. So, it's an interesting experience to have Chasids visit Magda's. Some of them are spying on each other. But, another is really nice. Working at Magda's is like sociological field research for me: I learn a little about how Chasids live their lives in general, and a lot about what some of them do that is outside of the norms of their own community.

Back to School

An entire chapter will be devoted to my formal schooling. For now, I'll just mention again that in September 1990, after I've worked about 9 months for Magda, I enroll as a freshman at Kingston College, the most selective liberal arts college in the Gotham University system.

I know I will need all of my energy to be available for my boys, work for Magda, and still do well in school. Three days a week spent at Magda's is what makes it all possible.

After matriculating at Kingston College for 4 years, I need only one more course to graduate, which I take and pass the following semester. I would have finished on schedule, but mother dies in early 1994, so I reduce my course load while I handle family matters. Nonetheless, I graduate *summa cum laude* with a BA in psychology.

As discussed, dating men socially isn't important to me during this period of my life. My goals are to care for my sons, feel better about myself, and become a psychotherapist — all the while standing on my own 2 feet.

(Not-Just-Talk) Therapy

Naturally, sex work isn't what I'd have chosen if there were any other way of escaping the poverty trap I was in (while maintaining my personal independence). But since it's just a temporary expedient, most of the time I'm okay with it.

Another reason I can accept it is that I feel I'm doing therapy. I always look at the men as human beings who have unmet needs. It's not just about physical contact. It's also about emotional connection. Some readers may be skeptical, but a surprising number of men will pay a good sum of money just to have a sympathetic younger woman (often in her 30's or 40's) listen to them talk about their life.

Because I was abused by father, the whole sex thing has always seemed to me kind of abstract, in the sense that sex has never felt like it has anything to do with who I actually am. So, I don't feel I'm losing anything, in that sense, by working at Magda's. Whatever meaning sex *could have* had for me as an adult was taken away when I was still a child.

NYC subway.

I'm repeating myself because so many people wonder, *How can anyone do this for a living?!* The answer is that working at Magda's completely changes my life. I'm able to go to college, which gives me hope that I'm not doomed to be old and poor in America. Winding up poor is a great fear of mine. It could well have happened. Many immigrants, as well as native-born Americans, are poor in NYC. Back then, I see poor people everyday on the subway. And, these days, the number of people living on the streets is rising again.

I know that I need all of my energy and all of my strength to lift myself out of poverty. I'm getting very little help from other people. So, I realize that escaping poverty is going to be almost entirely up to me. That is how it has always been in my life — if anything is to really change, I have to be the one who changes it.

Trouble in Paradise

I continue working at Magda's until sometime in 1993, when a less-discreet operation opens on the floor just above us. Unfortunately, things soon go downhill. Seedy looking men are now coming into the building. All kinds of things are being left in the hallway that shouldn't be there — such as condoms. Understandable complaints from ordinary tenants bring unwanted attention from the authorities. One day the bell for the outside door rings, and agents of the NYC Buildings Department come in.

NYC doesn't usually send uniformed cops or undercover detectives to close down a quiet place like Magda's. Instead, a Buildings Department inspector arrives and issues a summons for a laundry list of building code violations. For instance, the showers, sprinkler system, emergency exit, etc, aren't up to code. There are always things they can find — because the NYC Buildings Code has so many regulations.

There's a silent understanding that under-the-radar businesses, like Magda's, won't contest a civil summons. This way, no one is charged with a crime, so no one winds up with a criminal record. Technically, there are several days or a week to correct the violations. But, correcting them would be pointless, because the agents would just find more violations. Instead, the business uses this time to move to another location. Or else the owner, having gotten tired of all the hassle, retires from the business altogether.

In short, Magda has to close her place. I feel devastated, because Magda's has been my salvation. I've met some really nice guys there, and some have been my regulars.

For example, a Lufthansa pilot who comes periodically. Or, an art dealer (probably in his 70's) who lives in France, and stops by Magda's when he's New York. I have many positive memories, so I'm sad when Magda shuts down.

I'm also afraid. What's next? I don't know what I'll do!

Ally's: A Darker Shade of Pink

It's early summer 1993, and I've just signed up for more classes at Kingston College. Martie, one of the girls I knew at Magda's, suggests I come to work where she is now: Ally's. It's a *typical* brothel (unlike Magda's), located on Lexington Avenue in the 20's. Martie says I'd only have to be there 2 or 3 nights a week.

But the thought of working at Ally's scares me. I've heard through the grapevine her place is sometimes dangerous. Ally does have a security guard who checks every man who comes in, to see if he's a policeman — or a creep with a weapon. But, the fact that she finds this necessary is itself a troubling sign. Plus, any man can just call and make an appointment. There's no prescreening, as there was at Magda's. Some clients use cocaine, and are already shaking when they arrive! It's definitely not as safe as Magda's.

However, Martie assures me that Ally's really isn't that bad. She says she can handle it, and it'll be okay for me too. Since I don't know what else to do, I call Ally and go in for an interview. When I get there, I'm taken to the bathroom, where my arms are inspected to see if I'm injecting drugs. Ally herself has been in recovery in Narcotics Anonymous for several years. I tell her that I'm in recovery as well, and that I still have some scars on my arms from my past heroin use. But, they're obviously old scars, so she says, "That's fine — not a problem."

I take 2 or 3 day-shifts, which run from 9 AM to 5 PM. (Ally also has a night shift from 5 PM to midnight, which is much later than Magda's night-shift ran.)

Another Country

Almost everything is different at Ally's. Ten to 12 girls work each shift. We're a varied group, with ancestors from Africa, East Asia, Europe, Latin America, and the Middle East (a reflection of the diversity of New York City). Ages range from 18 to about 50. (At this point, I'm in my mid-30's.)

Unlike Magda's, at Ally's girls lounge about in a big room. Many wear provocative clothing. Some are semi-nude. Men come into the room, look the girls over, and then choose.

At Magda's, there were 4 or 5 separate rooms. When a client arrived, if he didn't request his regular girl, Magda would bring him into an available empty room. She'd tell him how many girls were there — usually 3.

Then, one at a time, each girl would enter the room and say, "Hi, my name is ____. Nice to meet you." We didn't converse further, and we weren't allowed to bargain or ask for additional money (unlike at Ally's).

Magda would return to the room, and ask the client which girl he'd like to spend time with. She'd then leave the room and inform the girl. It was always handled tactfully. We never felt we were being inspected as if we were a cut of meat.

Ally's place is run very differently. The girls are "on display" from the start. The client is brought into the living room, where typically 10 to 12 girls are lounging or walking about — doing whatever. The client can ask a girl's name and a few other questions, and then he chooses the one he wants to spend time with.

I'm one of the quiet ones. I sit there with either a textbook or my knitting. Yvonne, who is African American, also brings her knitting. We become friends, and sit there minding our own knitting, literally.

Also unlike Magda's, at Ally's some of the girls aren't to be trusted. They might steal anything. One time, someone takes my child psychology textbook. I think to myself, *Are you kidding? Someone stole my child psychology textbook!*

I know that no one else at Ally's is in school at the time. Maybe whoever took it is interested in child psychology — because many of the girls at Ally's have issues that may be connected to childhood trauma, or they have a child or children of their own.

Since anything left out of sight might quickly disappear, I soon learn to keep a handbag with personal items such as wallet, cosmetics, textbooks, etc, near me at all times. I always take them, and any other of my belongings, with me when I go into a session.

Another difference: In Ally's lounge area there are girls who are strutting about in outfits that would get them arrested if worn in a regular hotel lobby. A further difference from Magda's is that few of the girls at Ally's have goals beyond getting through to the next day. Of course, some girls do; but many don't. A lot of the girls at Ally's, if they make $1,000 in a night, spend it on partying with drugs, or on designer clothing, or a Gucci handbag, or supporting a boyfriend or pimp.

House Arrest

Sometimes Ally's is raided by *real* police (not Buildings Department inspectors). The neighbors know what's going on. They call 911 and say there's someone in the building with a gun (to get the police to show up).

When the cops arrive, they literally use a sledgehammer to break down the door! They destroy the whole place, turning everything upside down and throwing it around.

One time, I'm in a room just about to start a session with a client who is already undressed. When I hear police with their sledgehammers pounding on the outside door. I tell the client, "I'm really sorry, but *the cops* are coming." Then I leave — while he's still in the nude!

I join the other girls, who are now all sitting in the living room, feigning innocence. Plainclothes cops come busting through our door. They are very intimidating — screaming and yelling at us as if we are a band of terrorists brandishing assault rifles and hand grenades. They arrest 4 or 5 girls, pointing at them and shouting, "You, you, you — come with us." For some reason I'm never arrested, even though the police raid Ally's at least 3 times while I'm there.

Sociological Research

When I'm still somewhat new to Ally's, I walk into the reception area one evening while Martie, my friend from Magda's, is on the phone describing to a prospective client the dozen or so girls who are there that night — blondes, brunettes, redheads, busty, slim, etc. Debbie, a girl sitting nearby, is playing with herself in front of the rest of us as if this is perfectly normal. I think, *Omigod — this place is crazy!*

When Debbie sees me come into the room, she asks me to fondle her breasts so she'd reach orgasm. I won't do it, but I remember thinking, *I'll treat this as a sociological research project, like a participant field-study. It'll be a learning experience, to better understand what goes on in a brothel.* (Up until then, I really have no idea what a regular brothel is like, because Magda's was so different.)

I don't know if Debbie achieves her goal, because I quickly leave the reception area, and go into the living room where everyone else is hanging out.

There's a whole box full of sex toys in the reception area. Several of the younger girls, 2 or 3 at a time, would take toys into one of the rooms and pleasure each other. Meanwhile I'm sitting in the living room studying my child psychology textbook. I'm not into girls, and I'm not into watching. I just want to take care of my children and do well in school, while being at Ally's as little as possible.

Ally's Girls — A Sampler

Ally definitely has a diverse mix of girls, including some who are shouldering heavy responsibilities. One of them, Rita, is young, maybe 18 or 19. Her older sister has died from AIDS, leaving Rita as the head of her household. She now supports her mother and some siblings.

Rita gets pregnant, but continues working at Ally's into her 9th month. As her pregnancy proceeds, Rita becomes increasingly popular with clients. I can't understand why she is gaining in popularity — or why she'd often entertain 5 or 6 clients in one night while she's pregnant with her 1st baby.

Then there's Roxanne, who's also very pretty. She has piercings in all her erogenous zones, and she'd parade around without underwear. She might start dancing on a table in the living room — *really sexy dancing.* Other girls would start dancing with her. Soon they are simulating sex. (Some male fantasies about brothels do actually happen.)

Malina is about 19, naturally blonde, with the biggest blue eyes. Rita, Roxanne, and Malina often hang out together.

Cassandra is a tough Jamaican girl whose skin is as smooth and dark as the night. She calls me, "You f**king Austrian mountain bitch." (I like her.)

I think Cassandra is very sexy. She's tall and slim, with a breast size about 34A. But she's not flat-chested — in fact, she's beautifully proportioned. Then one night she comes to work with breast implants. She suddenly has huge breasts — DD or maybe E.

I can't understand why Cassandra did this. I think she already had a perfect body. Now her figure has lost its sense of proportion. She explains to me, "I have to compete with you, Austrian mountain bitch. You're white and blonde. It doesn't matter if *you* have a chest or not. But when you're black, you have to do whatever you can to make money."

This makes me sad. Up until then, I didn't know that black escorts aren't that popular with clients in America. In the Alpine region where I was raised, black people were still relatively rare. So over there, black women and men are romantically desirable. The situation for blacks is the opposite here. There are some really beautiful black girls at Ally's, and I feel bad that sometimes one of them would sit there for the whole shift and not get a session. Considering the overall context, this is very hard on a girl's self-esteem.

Mean Pimps and the Girls Who Love Them

While most of Magda's girls stayed with her a long time, at Ally's many girls just come and go. As noted, some have no particular plans for the future. Others may be there as part of the rotation in someone else's trafficking operation.

For example, one pimp controls rotating groups of girls from the Midwest. Three or 4 of them would travel together, working at Ally's for a month. Then they'd travel to a different city. Another group of girls, from Boston, are taking orders from a pimp based there.

This Boston pimp is really bad. He's well known in the body-building community as a trophy-winner. (While his crew of girls is in NYC working at Ally's, he sometimes makes them street-walk as well!)

These girls are young and beautiful, and because he makes them work out at the gym every day, they're in excellent shape. He demands that they eat healthy foods, and he doesn't allow them to smoke, drink, or use drugs, nor even to go clubbing.

They must tell on each other if one of them is doing something he forbids. He'll severely beat a girl who breaks any of his rules. But they're all madly in love with him, and would do anything to please him! (I'm dumb-founded by the whole thing.)

There's also a crew based in Michigan. While there, they work as strippers. Their pimp also sends them to New York to work in brothels. One of his girls (who has a baby) comes to Ally's so beaten up that she has a purple eye and bruises all over her body. She went to a club with some of Ally's other girls after work one night and another girl in her crew reported it. So the pimp flew from Michigan to New York and beat the stuffing out of her.

Not Free to Choose

In a brothel, the client gets to choose — the girls don't ordinarily have a say in the matter. There are plenty of times a girl hates to see a certain client, but she has to see him anyway. Does she give him the time of his life? Well, probably not. It's more likely that she just wants to get it over with — and it shows. And yet, for some men it seems that this is good enough. At times, I'd wonder to myself, *Why would they choose a girl who they already know doesn't want to be with them?*

Then again, sometimes we are *more* attracted to someone who doesn't reciprocate. And this happens with both men and women — it's part of the human dilemma. I've been pretty lucky in this respect. There are some clients that I really don't like to see. Fortunately, for the most part, these clients don't request me a 2nd time. In spite of exceptions, most men who pay for adult-companionship want to be with a woman who is warm and friendly. Even if she obviously feels no lust for him, he'd rather be with someone who doesn't treat him in a cold and distant manner.

As mentioned, I always look at a session as part therapy and part sociological research. I get good at asking a lot of questions to learn about a client's family, work, and other personal matters. And, by engaging him in conversation, I can spend most of our time giving him a regular massage.

Some men don't like this approach, but those who do are the ones who become my regulars. They enjoy having more than just physical contact. So that's only a small part of our session, which is fine with me. I need to conserve my energy for my 2 children, my day job, and school. If I'd let myself enjoy the physical part, I'd have felt bad about it afterward. I'm not there to have a good time.

Life Lessons

I learn a lot in this business by taking on so many different roles — an actress for the client seeking novelty, a nurse for those in emotional pain, a therapist for the ones needing a non-judgmental listener, and a friend for the lonely.

Plus, as noted, for the 1st time I learn how to relate to women. Because mother left when I was 5, I wasn't able to learn from her. Nor, from my Aunt Martha living next door. Now that I'm in this business, I'm finally at ease with other women.

In addition, I learn a good deal more about men. How gullible they can be. How important sex is to them. How what's between their legs is their be-all and end-all. For me, this aspect is new. Of course, having had several men in my life, I knew about male lust generally. But, I had no idea that they want so much *special* attention paid to what's "down there". (I'd never really given it much thought before.)

I also learn that I have to play the game, to act the part. The more experienced men know that it's an act, yet they still crave it. For many men, it's just a good fantasy, a pleasant form of escape and relaxation. Whether they're lonely, or just want some fun, or diversity, or novelty, they're happy to pay for the freedom to indulge their longing — without any strings attached.

Further, I get the inside scoop. Contrary to the sensationalism of the mainstream media (and certain well-meaning activists), I find most of the girls in the business are neither drug addicts nor being mistreated by clients or a pimp.

To be sure, everyone has their issues. There *are* girls who've been sexually abused (including myself). But, in most cases, we're treated a lot better by the clients than by husbands or boyfriends. The men we choose ourselves tend to be "hot" — and they know it. Clients, especially the more mature ones, usually realize they're clients precisely because they aren't a hunk. So, they tend to try harder to please. And of course, an hour a week, or even a few times a week, is not too long for a man to be on his best behavior. In a committed relationship, there's much more face time, and so more opportunity for stresses and strains — and abuse.

Thus, I learn a lot more in this business than I learned in regular jobs, like baking pizzas and calzones, selling clothing, or renting out apartments.

Angela's

I'm okay with Ally's (except for the police raids, which are scary). A few days after cops would close her place, she'd reopen. Soon she'd be shut down again. However, eventually, the authorities shutter her business for good.

I hadn't planned on being there for a long time anyway. In fact, after I've been at Ally's for only a few months, Magda calls me and says that Angela has opened her own place. Magda is in some way partnered with Angela, and asks me if I want to work there.

Angela's place is very much like Magda's, and many of Magda's former clients are now clients of Angela's parlor. I leave Ally's and start working for Angela. (Things are okay for awhile, until Marco comes into my life. More on him later.)

Soon Angela acquires a 2nd location in the neighborhood. This new spot has a swimming pool. Candy Man, who has transitioned from Magda's, loves to spend time in the pool, sometimes 3 or 4 hours while there. Most of this time is spent in conversation — he's a very lonely man. There are a number of clients who aren't there to have sex. As noted, they just want to have an empathetic woman listen to them talk about their life.

The Therapeutic Touch

Years before he became my client, Mel discovered his wife, the mother of their 3 children, was secretly working as an escort.

After he found out what she'd been up to, they arrived at a compromise (more below). But, Mel fell into a depression over the situation. He started overeating as a way to self-medicate.

Then his wife died in an auto accident. After a few years of not having any sex (and curious about the hidden world his wife had worked in), he started dating escorts himself.

By the time we meet, Mel weighs over 400 pounds. Other escorts have been repelled by his girth, but I don't judge him for it. I make him feel at ease, instead of undesirable.

Soon Mel soon tells me that I'm giving him reason to hope for happiness, and that he's begun working on his appearance and overall health. He's starting to feel he's not the ugly person that he'd thought, because I'm making him feel attractive and desired.

Over the 2-year period that he's my client, Mel loses about 150 pounds(!) Early on, we'd meet at an old hotel in Times Square. It isn't a bad place, but it's seen better days. However, as he begins to feel better about himself, he wants to explore nicer venues. We start to meet at boutique hotels, the trendy Hotel Z, or a new one in Battery Park where he gets us a nice suite overlooking the Hudson River. And, we begin spending much of our time together taking walks, or riding in a horse-drawn carriage in Central Park.

Through hard work, Mel is stage manager of a famous Broadway theater when we meet. He gets me tickets to shows there. Later, he becomes project manager for the construction of a jazz emporium at one of NYC's most prestigious addresses. Mel invites me to walk through the project while it's still under construction. (I have to wear a hard hat.)

Unfortunately, Mel falls in love with me. He's a really good person, and I do care about him as a friend. But, I don't have romantic feelings for him. We've shared wonderful times and had some great conversations. Even if he weren't paying me, I might have dined with him from time to time (as with other clients who have become just social friends).

But, I'm raising 2 sons and finishing up my education. And, by now I'm doing an unpaid internship as a social worker (while still escorting to make ends meet). To be honest, if it weren't for the money, there wouldn't have been nearly as much time in my busy schedule for dining with Mel.

When a client develops romantic feelings for me (clients fall in love with an escort more often than many readers might imagine), I feel guilty that, though not intending to, I may have led him on. And, these situations are always emotionally awkward. Mel is aware that I'm not interested in him romantically, and I worry that he may think I'm repelled by his weight. (I hope he realizes that this isn't the case.)

To avoid hurting him further, the next time he calls I explain why I'll no longer be seeing him. He responds, "You've probably always thought of me as a "John". But regardless, you have no idea how much you've helped me. And, how much you have enriched my life, even though it's all been a fantasy on my part, while for you just business. But it doesn't matter, because you've given me so much."

We then have an exchange of emails, which I've copied here (with minor edits for spelling and continuity):

> My Dearest Marlena,
>
> I do not think that you fully appreciate the importance and significance you have had in my life. It is I who am indebted to you.
>
> When I found out that my wife had been unfaithful to me, I was devastated. She was escorting not for financial need — I have always been a good provider. She did it for the excitement. She justified it by saying, "You are always working, you do not care for me, do you know what YOUR boys did (ie, I

wasn't there for them)...I am not your maid...Men are pigs and want only one thing...", etc.

My wife and I reached an understanding. She would quit escorting, and I would not divorce her, or tell her parents and friends. She would continue to be a loyal and devoted mother — but being a "wife" was optional.

This was very hard for me because I absolutely believe in the institution of marriage and the responsibility of child care. I wanted my children to have a childhood, one that I never had because of my father's heart condition and the fact that I always worked, from 6 years old stuffing church bulletins, construction at 12, and working in a slaughter house at 14 — the job I still have nightmares from occasionally.

Nothing in the world is more important to me than my children, and that is what I see in you above all else, your devotion and love you have for your boys. I have always believed that having children is the ultimate responsibility. This principle you have demonstrated in your life and know it only too well. For all that you have done for your family you have my deepest respect and admiration.

My physical relationship with my wife was meandering prior to her death, because I never was able to allow my heart to heal properly. Intimacy with her was never the same, and I had accepted that it would never again be what I thought it was.

Going to the internet for a "date" was not such a hard decision for me after several years of celibacy [after his wife died]. It seemed a safe way for uninvolved physical gratification. I stopped surfing the internet when you and I started our "New York City Tour". I have never been back to the adult-meet-up sites since. I almost went back, prior to writing this note to you, but decided against it.

(Do you remember we used to meet at the Tesla Hotel? That was because it was the safest, most convenient and cheapest hotel for me to utilize because of my work schedule.)

It does not matter if your website is up or down, and it does not change my feelings for you. Your radiant smile, your beautiful hair, your air of dignity and class, the ability to make me feel handsome, desirable, and as if I were the most important person to you, the storm of golden hair on the bed sheets, this is what I carry in my mind and heart about you.

I cannot imagine how repulsed you must have been by me when I was so heavy. But you still always made me feel special to you. My ability to come out from behind the "shield" of so much weight was due to you. I had somebody I wanted to be desirable for. I will always be indebted to you for that.

I am not a handsome man. And I have never thought of myself as a "great lover", especially since my issues with my wife (the expectation of male performance and all that). So I allowed myself to become obese as a form of protection against intimacy. But you always have made me feel special and that my physical inadequacies were not an issue with you.

I am sorry for this rambling letter. Let me get to it. You have been trying for some time to let me know that I was crowding you. I have not made it easy for you, and for this I apologize.

I have several requests that I hope you will honor. They are:

1) I was going to offer you tickets to *Man of La Mancha* for your birthday. It is playing at the Al Hirschfeld Theatre, also known as the Martin Beck, at 302 West 45th Street. The play is a little bit hokey, but the signature song "To Dream the Impossible Dream", performed by Brian Michael Stokes, is something I want you to hear. I can have four tickets left at the box office in your name if you want. You can send me the date and nothing more (no face to face). The tickets will be there.

2) Work on your clinical program and yoga. It becomes you.

3) Be kind to yourself — you are a very special lady.
I will always carry you in my heart and best thoughts....
I will always be there for you.........

Much love always,

Mel

My reply:

Dear Mel,

I am very touched by your words. It makes me sad that you think I have been repulsed by you. Believe me that was never the case!!! The extra weight made it a little more difficult to perform, maybe. But I never felt bad being with you!

Please believe that I always saw the kind, warm, and wonderful man that you are. Besides that, you are a wonderful lover and have always made me feel good and special!

Watching you lose all that weight was quite amazing. I know you worked very hard at it, and I am happy to hear that I have been a little bit of help and support for you.

I really do not want to lose contact with you. You have become very dear to me, and I care about you a lot. Thank you for sharing part of your life story with me. It must have been very difficult for you to deal with your wife's secrets. I give you a lot of credit for having handled it the way that you did.

My main reason for working as an escort has of course been money. However, there are other components and reasons why women choose this lifestyle. I know that for me it also has a lot to do with my childhood. My father was very difficult and abusive, and life with him was always unpredictable. On the other hand, he was a good provider and we never had money problems.

Even though my life in NYC was very difficult financially before I entered this business, I know that it is not only the money that has kept me in it for so long. In a strange way, I have recreated a safe childhood with different father figures (meaning clients), without having to relinquish control or losing my freedom.

Also, this business has certainly helped me a lot in terms of having more time for my children when they were younger, like going to Johan's baseball games and hockey games, and being able to afford a more or less middle class lifestyle, with occasional vacations and trips. This would have been impossible on my day job salary alone.

And, it helped me with getting my education. I spent about ten years in school between undergraduate and graduate studies. Being able to make more money in less time certainly helped to keep my life's anxieties at a lower level.

I am very grateful for this opportunity, but it also has left me fragmented and unable to have a relationship with one man. In 1995 I did get married and gave this business up completely. (I do believe in monogamy in a relationship and/or marriage). But it became another abusive situation. It ended with a separation in 1997, and a divorce in 2000.

That's when I started my website. It's almost three years later, and I'm struggling with the changes that I'd like to make in my life. I really want to leave this business and focus on my work, and maybe be able to have a normal relationship one day.

Warmest regards,

Marlena

Mel has stayed in touch with me. One of his son's has gotten into the US Naval Academy. The other son is doing fine too. His daughter is still in school, and functioning well. I like to think I've helped Mel in his own struggles.

Incidentally, I *don't* think of my clients as "Johns". I realize there are some women who are really hurting in the business, so they call clients "tricks" or Johns, and say other mean things about them. But I never feel that way. I look at these men as human beings who need help that I'm able to provide, and I feel their need should be respected. (Naturally, there are a few clients who are obnoxious, and I wind up disliking them. But, they are rare.)

My clients are getting the attention they aren't able to find elsewhere; attention that helps them and doesn't harm others. Most importantly, they get understanding and acceptance. In this sense, I feel that my work is important. It never feels sleazy to me (even though some of the girls at Ally's can be vulgar at times).

I think that there is also a spiritual component in our work. For many readers, this may sound misguided. But, I feel my work with these men is emotionally therapeutic. As an adult-companion, I don't just touch a man physically. I also lift his spirit. In that sense, it's like being a psychotherapist. Though called "sex work" by the media, it's more than just sex. It's also about how these men feel about themselves when they leave, in contrast to how they felt about themselves when they arrived.

Similarly, in my current life I don't look down on my psychotherapy clients (as some therapists do with a few of their clients). In both professions, I look at my calling as helping people who have an unmet need. Maybe, as with Mel, a man needs an escort because he weighs 400 pounds and is lonely. Or, maybe a psychotherapy client is unaware that she keeps reliving a childhood trauma. There's a lot of overlap between these professions — both are about emotionally comforting clients. However, the older profession adds the element of physical touch.

But I Still Have to Pay for Food and Rent

As an escort, I experience it as a privilege to be able to help a man who is lonely. But the catch is that I have to charge him for my time — just as I now have to charge clients for psychotherapy. I sincerely want to help my psychotherapy clients too. Yet, after their 45-minute session is over, even though sometimes a client may be depressed and crying, I still have to send them home — and charge them a fee. (Most of my psychotherapy clients are on Medicare or Medicaid, and I don't ask them for a co-pay.)

𝕸𝖆𝖗𝖈𝖔 : 𝖙𝖍𝖊 𝕳𝖚𝖘𝖇𝖆𝖓𝖉 𝕱𝖗𝖔𝖒 𝕳𝖊𝖑𝖑

From Book I:

> [O]n January 7, 1994, mother is working [as a flight attendant] on a trip from Washington's Dulles Airport to Columbus, Ohio. It is a freezing cold night, and there is an ice storm. It is a small plane. A lot of airports in the region have closed because of the weather. They fly anyway. The wings freeze and the plane crashes while attempting to land in Columbus. There are only 8 people on board, 5 of whom are killed, including the pilot, the co-pilot, and mother. She would have been 59 in March.

> After mother dies, my attendance at Narcotics Anonymous meetings becomes sporadic. When I do go to an NA meeting, I feel isolated. I focus almost all of my time and energy on my sons, work, and school. I don't want to deal with much else.

But Tracie, a friend from NA in Queens, keeps saying to me things like, "You haven't gone out since your mom died. You can't just stay home — it's not good for you. There's an NA conference in Maryland next month. Let's go to it."

Tracie continues nudging me to go with her. Finally, I agree. While we're there, I run into Darla, a friend from my early days in recovery when I was living in Maryland with mother and my sons. Darla is there with her boyfriend, Marco.

I immediately get a bad vibe from Marco. He seems kind of sneaky, and I don't trust him. (Looking back, I wish I'd followed my gut instinct.) But he's Darla's boyfriend, so I don't give him another thought. Tracie and I soon return to Queens. That's my 1st encounter with him. Nothing special.

Some Enchanted Evening

I start going with Tracie once in a while to "sober dances". In other words, there's music and dancing, but no alcohol. (I've been off drugs for 5 years by then.)

In June of that year, Tracie and I begin going to a country club in Forest Hills where 1 night a week it's alcohol-free. This club has a pool that we can swim in till midnight. One evening, I see Marco there. I ask him, "Where's Darla?"

He answers, "We aren't together anymore. She had a nervous breakdown, and she's been hospitalized." We start conversing about her condition.

Imago

It's odd how an event in the present can bring us back to an earlier time in life. After mother dies, it's almost as if I were 5 years old again. She has just abandoned us, and it's only father and me. Since this past Christmas, mother has gone from my life *again* (we had been growing closer), but this time for good.

In many ways, Marco has a personality similar to father's. Like father, Marco has a presence about him, and he's charismatic. He's also very controlling. But, at the start, Marco goes about it in a charming manner.

As noted, I saw red flags the 1st time I met Marco. Yet when I see him at the sober dance, I ignore the flags. We keep talking, and then start dancing. Soon we're dating.

We get much too close, much too quickly. But, I ignore my instincts, and a week or 2 later, Marco is moving into my house! I soon realize that Marco is personality disordered, narcissistic, infantile — all of it. But, I'm in a very vulnerable place, because mother died just months earlier.

Looking back, I think I was doing what I knew best — what I'd learned in childhood. When mother left father, I was stuck with a man who was in many ways immature and abusive. But, in spite of all of father's issues, he was the only one I could turn to at the time. (And he never failed to be there for me.)

At some level, I recognize these same personality disorders in Marco. But, according to Imago relationship theory, we often become romantically involved with someone who reminds us of the parent of the other gender (ie, their image, or in Latin, *imago*), because we (naively) hope this new person will heal the emotional wounds that the parent has caused.

So, as when I was with father (or with Joe), I'd do things that I know aren't helping me, but that I think will appease and calm Marco. Somehow, I imagine, this will make Marco change and become a nicer person. But, although I try again and again to appease him, Marco doesn't change (nor did father or Joe).

Plus, after mother died, perhaps I did need someone else to take charge. Maybe I'd have been completely at sea otherwise. All the emotions I felt when mother 1st left have recurred now that she's dead. Both times, I feel unable to stand on my own, with no one to defend me, no one by my side — abandoned, alone, and overwhelmed.

However, at least father was well established and provided me with a sense of security. I always felt safe with him. Nothing bad could happen to me (except he himself was hurting me). But he protected me from everything and everyone else — it was all very twisted.

Admittedly, Marco is somewhat similar that way — there's safety to being with him. But, I have to completely submit to him. So, once again, I lose my own identity. As with father, my needs are totally ignored by Marco. It's a very similar dynamic, except that father was successful and generous, whereas Marco is a loser and a sponge.

If I'd chosen a wealthy man who is controlling, at least I'd have been financially secure. But instead, I've chosen a lazy guy who is controlling nonetheless: lose-lose.

Invasion of Privacy

When I start dating Marco, Johan and Lukas are away at summer camp (something that working at Angela's has allowed me to do for them). It's while the boys are still away that I let Marco move in. He soon reveals himself as mean, jealous, angry, and arrogant. He's a user and a manipulator. In short, he's evil.

A few days after moving in, Marco goes through my photo albums, throwing out every picture with a man in it (including all the pictures of me with Joe). He invades my privacy further by examining my appointment book. He puts 2 plus 2 together, and realizes I must be escorting.

He then throws away my appointment book, and threatens to blackmail me. He tosses whatever else he dislikes into the garbage. I feel totally violated.

I can't believe I've gotten myself into this mess. In spite of all the therapy I've had, and everything (I think) I've learned, I've allowed another abuser into my life. Of all the men I've dated, he's absolutely the *worst* choice I could've made for a live-in partner. I know from the day he moves in that I've made a mistake — that I should never have allowed him to set foot in my house at all!

Now I can't get rid of him. I want Marco out of my life after only a week of his living under my roof. But he won't leave. He becomes threatening, saying things that really scare me. I don't know if Marco is telling the truth, but he says the scar on his forehead is a gunshot wound.

I'm absolutely petrified, and stop escorting immediately. I call Angela and explain, "I can't come in anymore. I have a boyfriend that I'm terrified of. He says he shoots people in the kneecaps, and that he's killed people in the past."

This is the one relationship I'm still ashamed of. Living with Marco is just plain wrong, because I'm exposing my children to a violent man. To this day, I feel guilty that I allowed it to happen.

But, I *am* really afraid of him.

Airport

Soon after Marco moves in, Lukas and Johan return from summer camp. Marco and I pick them up at LaGuardia Airport. While on our way there, my cellphone rings. Marco starts acting like a jerk: "Who's calling? Are you having sex with someone?" (He allows me no privacy at all, and it's making me very angry.)

At this time, I have an old Volvo station wagon that Raj — originally a client of mine from Magda's; now a good friend — gave me as a gift. (Raj is mentioned in Book I, but not identified as a former client.) It turns out my sons' flight has been delayed a couple of hours because of bad weather. So Marco and I are stuck waiting at the airport.

By the time the boys arrive and we've all gotten into the Volvo to leave the parking lot, Marco has made me furious. I floor the accelerator and smash through the wooden barrier at the parking lot exit, instead of stopping and paying the parking attendant. (I still remember the look of shock on his face.) I drive through all the red lights from LaGuardia Airport back home to Astoria.

Marco's Obsession

Marco thinks that *I'm* the one who's obsessed with black men, because of my affair with Joe. Whenever a black man is walking by, I have to be careful not to even glance at him, because otherwise Marco will have a fit. But, it doesn't always matter. Even if I *don't* look, Marco sometimes has a fit.

Marco's bad, *really* bad, and he brings out the worst in me. One time while he's driving our van (bought with proceeds from selling artwork Joe gave *me*; details to come) he suddenly starts yelling at me, "accusing" me of having looked at a black man (as if that were a crime). While he's yelling and screaming, and generally going crazy, I open the van door and jump out while it's still moving!

Another time, while parking in front of the house, I actually try to run over him. He jumps out of the way just in time. It's amazing that I don't kill him, or that he doesn't kill me.

It's a totally toxic relationship.

My Worst Decision Ever: *Marrying* Marco!

Instead of kicking him out the door after the 1st time he yells at me, I end up becoming even more boxed-in — by *marrying* Marco.

My 1st husband, James, marries me purely for love, while I marry him partly to become a legal immigrant. However, as noted, it's not a sham marriage. I feel genuine affection for James, we live together as man and wife, and I sincerely try to make our marriage work.

Yet, because of my past wounds from father's abuse, I can't handle marital intimacy. This leads to my divorcing James. Still, I do get my green card from our marriage. So, a part of me feels I should pass it forward by marrying Marco, so *he* can get a green card. (But at the same time, I'm terrified, because in my heart I know it's the wrong move for my family and me.)

In June 1995, a year after I run into him at the sober dance in Forest Hills, Marco and I marry. The marriage ceremony is a very simple affair. We don't even bring our own witness to Queens Borough Hall. Once we're there, we ask a complete stranger to be the witness to our marriage. Afterword, I don't tell anyone, not even my sons or my sister, Kim.

As I feared, marrying Marco is a terrible mistake. I feel trapped and scared to death that I will never be able to escape. At times I think, *This is it — I'm stuck with this man for the rest of my life. I can never get rid of him!*

It feels like doomsday. But, not just one final doomsday — doomsday every day for eternity. I'm frightened and paralyzed.

Twice As Many Teens

We're married less than a year when I suggest to Marco that his 2 teenage children come live with us. I'm not being purely altruistic. I feel that if his children live with us, perhaps he won't focus so much of his attention on me.

(Similarly, when I was a child I wished father would remarry and have more children. But, after mother left, he could never really love another woman.)

However, there's also an idealistic motive: Maybe, by helping raise his children, Marco will grow up and be more responsible in general.

So I say to him, "Your kids are at a vulnerable age: Sergio is 14 and Misa is 13. They haven't been learning to speak English. And now your ex-wife has remarried, and has her new husband's 2 kids to look after. You have more time for your 2 kids than she does."

In April 1996, Misa and Sergio move in with us. This *adds* to what I'm already putting my own kids through. First, there's this loser of a man who has been living with us. And now I'm moving both of his teenagers in too. Since Lukas is almost 18 and Johan is 14, there are suddenly 4 teens under the same roof competing for my time and attention.

As mentioned, I don't work for Angela anymore, because I'm terrified that Marco will kill me if I do. But, sex work has afforded me the time and money to earn a BA in psychology at Kingston College. On the strength of this, I'm able to get a job as a social worker at Manhattan Family Hospital. I work with children in foster care who have a history of being abused — physically and sexually.

Marco works as a house painter (when he works at all). If there are a few drops of rain, he doesn't go out on a job. I'd come home from my office and find him sitting in the bedroom watching television — playing the big king.

The arrival of Sergio and Misa does calm Marco down a bit. His attention is no longer solely on me. He now has his son and daughter on his mind (even though he basically does nothing for them). He's just another child himself, completely irresponsible.

Later in 1996, I enter a grad school program at Gramercy University. Along with my day job, this allows me to be away from Marco much of the time. Attending classes isn't my only distancing device. I stay up at night studying, waiting for him to fall asleep, so that I can go to bed without him trying to touch me.

While at Gramercy University, I write papers on what I've learned working at Manhattan Family Hospital. My Master's thesis is on their foster care program. In 1997, I receive a Master's degree in Public Administration.

The Last Straw

By then, Johan is 15 and Lukas is almost 19. Again, I've been feeling really guilty for creating problems for my sons by letting Marco come into our lives. Then one night in June, Marco and Johan get into a fight. Marco, who has a black belt in Taekwondo, kicks Johan in the chest.

That's when I go crazy on Marco, and tell him he has to go. He screams back at me, "I'm not leaving this house except in a body bag!"

Meanwhile, Johan runs out of the house to get a hammer. I say to myself, *Someone's going to die tonight if I don't separate these 2!*

So, I tell Johan to go to his friend's house and not return til I say it's okay. I call Lukas, and tell him to check in on Johan and make sure he's alright. Then I leave the house too.

I call our family therapist. (Because of Marco, my sons and I are back in family therapy.) I've already recounted to her that Marco is an abusive manipulator. She advises me, "You need to get help from the police."

I'm afraid of pressing charges — even though I know it's the right thing to do. But because so many women have been too afraid of their abuser to press charges against them, New York's laws on domestic violence have been reformed to allow law enforcement to independently decide whether or not to bring charges. In this case, when the detectives get to my house, they arrest Marco on the spot.

That night, with Marco out of the house, I pack all his stuff and put it outside on the porch. I tell his children that he's not allowed to come back inside.

The next day, Marco is released from jail and returns to the house. He's very angry, of course, but thankfully the police accompany him. I am granted an order of protection. Marco is no longer allowed to enter my house. But he takes the van, which I paid for, since he thinks he's entitled to it.

Although Marco's gone, his daughter and son continue living with me for awhile. I can't in good conscience ask them to leave, because Marco has been abusive to *them* too. For example, Marco threw his son on the floor, and then kicked him in his face and chest. I tell Sergio and Misa they can stay with me until they have other options. I want them to at least be able to finish high school.

So, it's a tough period, a really tough period.

Years of Stalking and Harassment

Now living in *my* van, Marco begins a campaign of stalking and other forms of harassment. It's very upsetting that at any time I can turn around and see him following me. Or find him lurking around my house. He might walk past me when I arrive home — just to let me know he's always shadowing me. Sometimes he'd suddenly pop up right behind me. When I arrive for work at Manhattan Family, he might be standing in the building lobby at the elevator.

Or, he might call the switchboard at my job. Everyone there knew not to transfer his calls to me. But he'd give them a made-up name, so he'd still be put through to me.

Even though I just hang up, he keeps coming up with crazy stories to try to get me to converse with him. For example, he might claim he's dying of AIDS to manipulate me into feeling sorry for him.

When that wouldn't work, he'd threaten me. When that too wouldn't work, he'd show up at my job and plead with me.

It feels like Marco's harassment will never end. He's absolutely relentless. He goes to each AA and NA meeting I attend in the area, and tells everyone in the room that I'm a prostitute. He calls the Human Resources department at my job at Manhattan Family, and even faxes them a letter, telling them they should fire me because I'm a sex worker.

A woman from HR calls me into her office for a meeting about this. To my relief, she reassures me, "I'm so sorry you have a husband who keeps calling and saying horrible things about you. I hope you're okay. We know what a good person you are. Don't worry, nothing's going to happen to your job. We're just sorry you're dealing with this man."

Change of Direction

In the meantime, I start to doubt that clinical social work is what I really want to do. After several years of trying to help clients one-on-one, I think I might be better suited for managerial work. Clinical work has been emotionally draining, because at Manhattan Family I'm mainly seeing kids who've been sexually abused. I've gotten a Master's in Public Administration, so I qualify for office work that would have some emotional distance from all-day contact with clients who are greatly suffering.

But, after a lot of reflection, I decide in the end to get a Master's in Clinical Social Work, and continue on the path of helping people face-to-face. I apply to prestigious Uptown University, get accepted, and enroll in September 1998.

While I'm at Uptown U, my Master's thesis supervisor, Letitia, shares with me that she too was stalked by her "ex". She'd wake up in the middle of the night because he was parked in her driveway flickering his car's headlights on and off. She felt terrified. Eventually the FBI got involved, and her ex wound up going to prison. But, she was terrified of him the whole time.

Learning that Letitia, an educated professional, had an experience so similar to mine is very helpful. Because of what she has confided, I don't feel like such a loser.

I tell my lawyer friend, Tim, that I want to stop Marco from getting a green card on the basis of our being married. Tim advises me to write a letter to INS (Immigration and Naturalization Services, since renamed Citizen and Immigration Services) explaining everything: Marco's violence, stalking, and general harassment; that I've had to get an order of protection from him; and that I want to dissolve the green card application I filed on his behalf.

I follow Tim's advice. Withdrawing my sponsorship feels empowering, because I've been so victimized in the past that with Marco I felt like a helpless child again. I should've annulled the whole marriage. But at least he hasn't gotten a green card through me (if at all), and I'm glad of that.

Getting Back to Business

Breaking up with Marco puts me and my sons back into poverty. My starting pay at Manhattan Family was $22,000. Although I now have a Master's degree in Public Administration, my salary is still only $27,000.

In the 1990's, the for-profit sector is rocking in New York City, so it's tough on my kids that we're just scraping by. Things were much better for them when I was working for Magda's, later Ally's, and then Angela's. Because I had the time, we could do fun stuff together like skateboarding and rollerblading. And with the added money, we went skiing a few times. We even went to Disney World.

Then I allowed this abusive fool Marco to take over my life, and all of a sudden we were poor again. After I'm finally rid of him, I ask myself: *How can 5 people (now including Marco's kids) live on $27,000 per year in New York City?!*

$27,000 a year is nothing in NYC with 4 teens — 3 boys and 1 girl — who are eating almost more than I can find time to shop for on a daily basis. They're constantly hungry, so I need to have a fridge full of food. Plus, I should be at home to monitor them so I know what they're up to.

I call Angela and ask her, "Is there any way I could work maybe 1 or 2 nights a week? I can't work really late because I have to be home for the kids. But, I leave Manhattan Family at 5:00. I can be at your place by 5:30. Maybe I could see a client and leave by 8:30 or 9 o'clock?"

Angela is very understanding. She allows me to come in for 2 or 3 hours, and she makes sure I get at least 1 client every shift. I work only 1 or 2 nights a week for her. Along with the $27,000 I'm earning at Manhattan Family, I make just enough to manage.

There's a lot on my plate. I'm still working full-time at Manhattan Family as a therapist for abused children, I'm back working for Angela for a few hours a week, I have 4 teens to care for, and I have Marco stalking me! *Plus,* other legal matters are pending (details below).

Cuba Sí — Marco No!

I want to learn Spanish, because fluency in Spanish is a necessity for social workers in NYC. (Also, I just like it.)

There's an interesting looking storefront I sometimes walk past on Broadway in Harlem. It has sort of a hippie-like appearance. A sign announces that Spanish classes are offered inside. One day, I decide to check it out. Reynoso, who is from Chile, and Antonia, his girlfriend from Venezuela, are teaching Spanish there as a couple. I sign up for a class.

Miriam and I meet in this class. She tells me she's in a program that's going to hold classes at the University of Havana for 2 weeks. I say to her, "Wow — I'd love to go to Cuba!"

Miriam replies, "Well then, *come!*"

Lukas is now 21. Technically he lives with me, but he stays mostly with his girlfriend. Johan is 17, and in high school. He still needs me to some extent, but not that much anymore. My sister, Kim, now lives with us. She's usually home when I'm in school, which is a big help. Misa moved out and is living with Marco in a place he found. Sergio has joined the Marines. So, the Cuba trip is a *go.*

When I get back from Cuba, Marco and I have a few conversations over the course of several days. I think, *Maybe I should give him 1 more chance.*

But it isn't even a week before he has one of his fits of jealousy — screaming at me and physically intimidating me. I soon come to my senses and (again) realize this relationship will never work. It's over.

Nevertheless, Marco continues to swear that he loves me. He gets a tattoo identical to the small one I have. While Sergio was still living with me, after he'd visit Marco, he'd return with presents for me from Marco. I get a CD from him with only 1 song on it: *You're Still the One,* performed by Shania Twain.

While Marco continues sending gifts to me, for a mad moment I again think, *Maybe.* Fortunately, I'm wiser now. I'm no longer thrown off-balance by his alternating between romancing me and threatening me. I've gotten a 5-year order of protection against him, so I feel a little bit safer than before. I tell Marco to stop calling me. (That's when he begins going around and badmouthing me to everybody.)

For the most part, though, he stops physically stalking me after I get the order of protection. But one evening in 2003 Miriam and I are, by chance, dining in the same restaurant as he is. Perhaps he's miscalculated, or is just ignoring, that the 5-year order of protection I got (a longer than normal period, because of his over-the-top persistence in harassing me) has 1 more day to run before expiring.

While Miriam and I are conversing, he comes up to our table, folds his arms in some sort of martial arts pose, and stands there shouting at me. Pretending not to recognize him, I say, "I don't know who you are. I'd appreciate it if you'd leave."

After Miriam and I finish our meal, I go to the police and report the incident. As a result, Marco is jailed again.

Even after that, Marco still comes to my office. And, he keeps harassing me in other ways, because he continues living in my neighborhood for a good while. Happily for me, he has moved away since then, so I haven't seen him in a long time. (I did see him once in recent years, peering into the window of a yoga studio I have by then in Astoria. More about the studio below.)

I also hear bad things about Marco from other people in the neighborhood. I learn that he's been beaten up at an NA meeting, because the people there hate him too. Another woman has gotten an order of protection against him. Yet another woman has kicked him out of her apartment. And, because he didn't pay his share of the rent, he has been beaten up by another roommate and kicked out of that apartment too. So, Marco causes trouble wherever he goes.

I'm grateful that I've been able to get rid of him for good. About a year ago, though, he calls me at my psychotherapy practice (the phone number is publicly listed, of course). He says he needs to speak to me. I recognize his voice, but reply, "Marco who?"

He responds, "You know who I am."

I answer, "I'm really sorry — I have no idea who you are. You must have the wrong number."

"No — this is Marco! You know who I am, Marlena. I need to talk to you."

"Sir, you're mistaken. I really don't know who you are. You have the wrong number." Then I hang up on him.

Sometimes, he tries to contact me on my birthday. For example, one year he texts me "Happy Birthday". I don't recognize the phone number. I text back, "Thank you. Who is this?" I get no answer. Then it occurs to me: *I'll bet it's him.*

I google Marco's full name. I find that he's now a taekwondo instructor and nutrition coach, with the same phone number as the birthday text's sender. Now I *know* it's him.

About 2 weeks later, he texts: "Are you still married?" (I marry a 3rd time; details below.) Again, I don't answer. A few days later, he texts: "I can't hear you" — with 5 exclamation marks. After 10 years of my not speaking to him at all, suddenly he's started sending arrogant, demanding texts.

A Lesson Learned

It's his way of trying to intimidate me again. But, I don't respond. Instead, I give his contact information to a male friend, who tells him to stop calling me if he wants to have a good life, or the like. Whatever the exact words of the warning, I haven't heard from Marco again. I learn from this experience that if I'm dealing with a bully, the only way he will stop is if someone stronger stands up to him.

This is a big lesson for me. I used to be more optimistic about people. I thought if you sit down and talk to *anyone* rationally, you could arrive at a reasonable outcome. I've learned, the hard way, this isn't always realistic.

I still blame myself for ignoring my initial gut feeling about Marco. In spite of warning signs from the outset, I got involved with him anyway. To re-emphasize: I still feel guilt for allowing this man to abuse me and my children.

𝕿𝖍𝖊 𝕬𝖗𝖙 𝖔𝖋 𝖙𝖍𝖊 𝕾𝖙𝖊𝖆𝖑

As mentioned, when Marco first moves in, he rummages through all of my belongings, without my permission. This is how he finds under my bed (where I'd all but forgotten them) drawings and paintings created jointly by Joe Kewl and myself, as discussed in Book I. Marco starts saying *we* should sell them to make money for *us* (because he assumes that whatever is mine is his too).

He just takes over everything, and I'm afraid to try to stop him. The good part is that we go through the process of cataloging all the drawings and paintings. Marco and a friend of his photograph and number each of the works. Marco then takes a few works to a major auction house, around 1996, and they sell a couple of the pieces.

Soon after that Morty, a Manhattan entertainment lawyer handling Joe's estate, sees some of the other pieces in the auction house's catalog. He contacts the auction house and tells them to block the sale of anymore of the artwork.

However, after the auction house gives him my contact information, Morty calls me and says, "Don't worry about it. I know you were in a relationship with Joe, and that he gave you the drawings. I'm faxing a letter to the auction house telling them I've okayed it. The proceeds are yours — not to worry."

I obtain my own copy of his fax, and the auction goes ahead as scheduled.

But, only 5 or 6 pieces sell — not nearly as many as I've been hoping. Still, I'm able to buy a van with the money. Yet, even though it's rightfully mine, the van is put in Marco's name — because that's how it is. At the time, I'm completely controlled by him. (So, after the police make Marco move out, he winds up with the van I paid for.)

Meanwhile, all the other drawings and paintings I did with Joe are still in the suitcase under my bed. I try a 2nd time at the same auction house. This time, none of the pieces sell.

I decide to try selling them on my own. I learn from an art magazine that some of Joe's other drawings are already being sold at a gallery in Soho.

The gallery is owned by Sylvia and her son, Mark. After getting in touch with them, I go to their gallery, and leave on consignment a couple of dozen of the pieces that are already framed.

Sylvia never calls to notify me when a piece has sold. I have to keep calling her to check. Early on, she admits to selling a piece here and there. But after she's denied having made anymore sales for some time, I decide to pick up the paintings and bring them home. I go to the gallery expecting to bring back 13 to 15 works that should still be there. But, Sylvia claims there are only 2 in the gallery. I ask her where are the rest of them? She says she doesn't know. I reply, "What are you talking about? You don't know?!"

She responds that Mark must have taken them to Florida. I tell her, "Look, I gave these works to you on consignment, and we have a written contract. So, you can't just move my paintings to another city without informing me — they're not your property. And, if you sell something, you have to let me know."

I later learn they have sold a number of my paintings without telling me — much less paying me anything. Instead, they claim they have no idea what is going on. Soon I can't reach them by phone or in person. For 2 months, I stop by the gallery from time to time, and am told that neither of them is there.

I call Mark in Florida. He gets arrogant and nasty with me over the phone. So, I contact my lawyer friend, Tim. He agrees to take my case.

Meanwhile, I put an ad for the artwork in the For Sale section of *Jazz News*, a magazine for enthusiasts. Dutch, an art dealer, contacts me from his base in Europe. He's intrigued, but wants to know how well I knew Joe. I explain that I went out with him for about 18 months from 1986 to 1987, and traveled with him to concerts he performed in, like the Montreux and New Orleans jazz festivals.

Having decided that I'm not one of those people who only imagines having had a relationship with a celebrity, Dutch flies to New York so he can examine the artwork in person. We meet at a hotel on the West Side of Manhattan. I have Lukas with me. (He's now a tall, strapping 20-year-old — like father at that age.)

I bring a suitcase full of drawings and paintings, and show Dutch maybe 60 or 70 pieces. I offer him a price for the whole collection, including the works I haven't brought. He says, "I'm very interested, but let me go back to Europe to think about it. In a week, I'll let you know what I can do."

Just a day or so later, Dutch calls me from Europe and offers me 30% less than my asking price. We do some haggling, and agree on a bit more than that. Within a week, he returns to New York and pays me the amount we settled on.

I'm thrilled! Most of the ones signed by Joe have already been sold at the auction house or the downtown gallery. But Dutch does get some signed ones, and he knows the unsigned pieces are authentic. He's done research on Joe's art, so he knows a genuine piece when he sees one.

Dutch goes back to Europe, and advertises the artwork on the internet. Soon I get a letter from Joe's estate, with a "cc" to Dutch. We are both being sued for copyright infringement, and for my having "stolen" Joe's drawings!

Debt Relief

It's a good thing that I got Marco out of the house before I received the money from Dutch. Marco has such a sense of entitlement that he'd have taken all of it. I'm really relieved that, with the help of the police, I've at least kept him at a distance from my home, family, and finances.

Getting this money is empowering, because I'm able to pay off a lot of debts. And the money provides some options going forward, like being able to do more things as a family. As mentioned, we were finally doing okay once I started working at Magda's. But, we went back to being poor during my years living with Marco, because he made me stop doing sex work — yet he was barely paying *his own* way.

Now that I'm in charge of my life again and have the money from the artwork, plus my day job and the extra income from Angela's, I'm able to do things with my children. It's like being able to breathe again, after being smothered for 4 years.

The Settlements

The lawsuit with the downtown gallery also gets resolved. They never account for what became of the missing paintings, nor specify how much they received for any that they sold. But, I'm able to prove which paintings were missing, because I have photographs of them all. The judge awards me a nice sum.

As my lawyer, Tim has been very supportive, and a really dear friend. I pay his legal fees, but the rest of the award is mine — and not Marco's! I feel like I'm finally having some successes in my life: I've gotten rid of Marco, and I've won the lawsuit with the sketchy Soho gallery owners.

And then there's the lawsuit with Joe's estate. It drags on for at least 2 years, because the estate is hoping to wear me down with their bogus lawsuit. They know they are absolutely wrong. As already mentioned, their lawyer sent a letter to the auction house stating that I'm the legitimate owner, and that I have the right to sell the artwork. Yet, a year later, when I place an ad in *Jazz News*, the same lawyer turns around and calls me a thief! On top of that, the estate sells one of Joe's works that I colored — and which has *my* initials on it along with his — without compensating me.

Then the auction house publishes a catalog in which the estate is offering other works by Joe, with a painting of mine on its cover! Tim says, "Let's counter-sue. They're infringing on *your* copyright."

So it becomes a long, drawn out affair. I counter-sue *pro se* (ie, I represent myself) because Tim's law firm is worried that I may not win a dime. But, Tim coaches me through the whole process.

For awhile I was dealing with 3 different legal actions (inclu-ding harassment by Marco). It was all very stressful. As noted, in 1998 I began studies at Uptown University that led to my Master's degree in social work. Dealing with these lawsuits during this period was distracting, time consuming, and draining.

But eventually Joe's estate's lawsuit is thrown out of court (because it's meritless) and that's the end of it. It's a great relief in 2000 when it's all over.

State Court, Foley Square, NYC.

Schule

As a child I felt insignificant in father's overwhelming presence. So I was unaware of the strengths I had. Looking back, I now realize I was a good student (prior to puberty). Studying was easy for me, and I learned quickly. I was very good at reading and writing (and my math was okay).

In Italy, children have 5 years of elementary school and 3 years of middle school. Then they (or their parents) choose which educational track they'll pursue — business, art, the humanities, or foreign languages.

But by the time I'm in 8th grade, I can no longer function academically. Between father's abuse at home, and my entering puberty, there's too much going on in my head — and my heart. Math suddenly becomes too difficult for me. Yet, I don't care anymore. I feel, *Who gives a damn?*

Val Gardena

After graduating from middle school, I don't know what to do next. Three years earlier, when I was 11 and she was 14, my cousin Astrid (the future mother of Cara) left our hometown of Bolzitano to attend art school in Val Gardena, a valley nestled in the Dolomites (a region of the Italian Alps further east). Val Gardena is famous for its many artists working there in various media.

Astrid has always been a role model for me. And, she's the only person in my life who consistently stands up to father on my behalf. (As a daughter of father's brother, she could get away with it.)

I decide that I want to enroll in the same art school. However, it's about a 2-hour drive from home. Father won't allow me to go, because it's too far away for him to completely control me (which is one of the things I most like about it). Father needs me to stay in Bolzitano to cook, clean, shop, and support him emotionally.

Liceo Scientifico

And so, art school is out of the question. The school that father does allow me to attend is a science academy (*Wissenschaftliches Lyzeum* in German, *Liceo Scientifico* in Italian), where physics, chemistry, biology, and math are taught. It prepares students for university if they intend to go into business, accounting, science, or even law.

But math and physical sciences aren't my strengths. I'm much better at art, literature, and physical education. I also do well in writing, history, geography, and the social sciences — all of which I love. In short, a science academy is the wrong school for me.

So now I'm in the 9th grade, and an emotional wreck. I'm in the midst of puberty. I hate myself, feel fat and ugly, and have no self-esteem. I'm constantly scared father will do something grossly inappropriate in private, or flip-out and embarrass me in public. It's a nightmare (and it will get much worse in the coming years).

I'm trying my best in school, but math is just not my thing. The math teacher would say things like, *Why don't you just go to the bar and have a beer and come back when the class is over?*

Teenage Wasteland

Café Odeon is a European-style diner/bar located in the center of Bolzitano. If, like me, you're young and feeling rudderless, Café Odeon is the place to hang out. It's there that I meet Fabio, another lost soul.

Now that I'm 14, I can't function academically or socially. I'm very depressed, so I start to self-medicate using street drugs like heroin (given to me by Fabio, who is then 17).

I'm getting no moral support from father, or anyone else. There is never any discussion about what *I* want to study, or what *my* goals are. No one ever says to me, "What are your interests?" Or, "What would you like to do when you grow up?" Instead, father decides that I'm to run a hotel that he'll build for me on his property. It's *his* goal for me.

My homelife is filled with constant conflict — fighting, yelling, and beatings by father. I'm with Fabio at Café Odeon the 1st time they meet. Father comes over to our table, and Fabio stands up to greet him. Father immediately punches Fabio in the face (not entirely without reason, as explained in Book I), breaking his nose and sending blood splattering everywhere.

It's a terrible time. I can't focus in class, much less study at home.

Father's concern about my using heroin, and my relationship with Fabio (who, as noted, is dealing drugs), eventually overcomes his need to have me under his constant control. After I'm arrested for possession of pot (while on a jaunt in Munich), he sends me to America to live with mother, who is now in a 2nd marriage. In only a month, she sends me back to him. But a month after that, he sends me to her again. This time I'm with mother for about a year, before being returned to him yet again.

Then mother comes to Bolzitano for a visit. (In spite of her marrying and divorcing twice more, and father's many girlfriends after she leaves us, their romantic ties continue to the end of his life.)

Her visit in my mid-teens is the 1st time either of my parents have discussed what I should do with my life. I tell her I want to go to art school to study graphic design. To her credit, mother helps me by looking into an art school in Munich. I've been working on an art portfolio, and this school likes my work.

But, the school rejects my application, since they require completion of the 10th grade, and I have credit only through the 8th grade. (Because of all my teenage turmoil, I didn't pass the 9th grade exams at *Scientifico Liceo*.) So, I'd first have to complete the 9th and 10th grades before my application to the art school could be considered.

After feeling completely lost during my year at *Scientifico Liceo*, it seems totally unrealistic to me to return there for 2 more years. So, now I don't know where to go — or what I'd do when I got there.

School for Scandal

I promised father that if I didn't get accepted to the graphic design school, I'd apply to the hotel management school in Bad Wiessee, a beautiful spa town about 30 miles south of Munich. This fits his plan to build a hotel for me to manage — so that he can continue to manage *me*.

In September 1976, I turn 18. The following month, feeling desperate to continue my education, I enroll in the hotel management school's 2-semester program. It's a way out — at least I won't have to live at home while I'm there.

It doesn't matter what my academic qualifications are. Virtually everyone who pays the fee is accepted to this school. Because the tuition is high, many of the students are from wealthy families (like me). They've spent their adolescence partying a lot, but not much else (also like me). So, we end up at this school.

I'm sure we learn something while we're there, but basically it's one big party. There are lots of kids with loads of money, not only from wealthy German families, but also from elsewhere in Europe, Africa, the United States — all over the world. It's drinking, drugs, and sex all the way through. I don't know how we even make it to our classes.

Double-F's

One student has the biggest breasts I've ever seen on a young woman. She must be an F or double-F — and she wears mini-skirts and high heels. We have an 11 o'clock curfew, but a few of us would tie together sheets and let her down from a window — like in a movie — so she could escape to be with her boyfriend. (At the end of the school year, she's 1 of the 3 girls who are pregnant.)

I'm so sad that I cry a lot. I have my own room, where I spend my time painting and drawing (since I really want to be in art school). But I do get through the program. This marks the end of my schooling in Europe. I don't return to school until 13 years later, after I've been living in America for awhile.

Instant Career

After graduating from hotel management school, I have no clear goal. But, the last thing I want is to work with father in *any* fashion — not in his restaurant (one of his several businesses), as he has talked about, and certainly not in the hotel that he plans on building. He has been my ball and chain since childhood. Working in this hotel he's planning would feel like life imprisonment.

Instead, I get back together with Fabio. Soon I'm pregnant with Lukas, and 4 years later our son Johan is born (both planned). Having babies with Fabio is my way out — a path to an instant career and purpose in life as the mother of 2 boys. It's also a way to escape from father's control and abusiveness. In retrospect, I think getting pregnant is what I needed to do at that time in my life. (My greatest pride is in how my boys have turned out as adults.)

Fast Forward

[For the sake of clarity, this subsection reviews events noted at the beginning of this volume. Following that is a summary of the period between my last schooling in Europe and the start of my schooling in the US.]

Father dies in 1980 leaving me (his heroin-addicted daughter) some plots of land in good locations, plus several buildings, apartments, businesses, motor vehicles, antiques, and paintings — an estate worth at least a few million dollars in today's money. In less than 3 years, the money is gone, I've dumped Fabio for cheating on me with my cousin Astrid, and I'm living with my 2 sons in my car.

Now living in the US with her 3rd husband, mother gets wind of the situation and comes to Italy, obtains legal custody of my sons (who are, after all, her grandsons), and takes them to America to live with her. She allows me to follow, so I can stay with them while getting help for my addiction. This is the one time that mother really comes through for me — and it changes the whole course of my life. If she hadn't rescued me at that critical point, I might well have died of a heroin overdose before very long.

Once here, I meet James in Narcotics Anonymous. We soon marry, so I get my boys back. But because of my unresolved issues with father, the marriage doesn't last long.

For a year and a half, I date the jazz great Joe Kewl. (Fortunately, I don't move in with him.) After enduring his ongoing emotional abuse, I catch him with another woman, which ends that relationship.

I then meet Carlos. Like James, he's a good man. And, he's a hit with my boys. Soon, he's living with us. He helps a lot financially, so for a time we aren't poor. But, as with James, because of father's abuse I grow to loathe Carlos's touch.

Carlos goes into rehab for his cocaine habit in fall 1989, which throws the boys and me back into poverty. This soon leaves me unable to feed myself and my children with the entry level jobs I've been stuck in due to having only an 8th grade academic education. But still, I can no longer live with Carlos. We separate when he gets back from rehab in early 1990, costing me the financial support he'd surely have resumed providing.

By now, I realize I'm not someone who can marry just for financial support (as mother has felt forced to do). It'd be absolute torture for me. I can't handle even being with a man that I *really like* on a daily basis! I surely can't handle *setting out* to find a man just to have him foot the bills for me and my sons. (This may seem ironic, because I wind up becoming an escort. But, an hour with a man is one thing; 24/7/365 with the same man is another thing entirely.)

And so, I have to figure out an escape route on my own — because there's no other way.

Back in 1987, after I break up with Joe, a friend puts up the fee for me to attend The Forum. It's a 2-weekend self-help program that definitely shifts something inside me.

Part of this program is to create a life vision. It's then that I realize my goal is to become a psychotherapist. A woman there says to me, "That's a long, tough road. You don't even have a high school diploma. You *can* do it, but it's not going to be easy, because it will take years and years of school."

When I hear her words, I make a firm decision: *I will go to school. I don't care how long it takes. One day I'll be done, and I'll have my degree. I'm going to focus on just getting an education, because I know I'm handicapped in terms of ever having a romantic relationship.*

However, it's not until 1989, while I'm still living with Carlos and have some financial breathing room, that I finally set out to get a GED. I take an evaluation test at Wagner Community College, to determine what prep classes I'll need before taking the GED test. I do well enough on the evaluation test that I don't need to take any prep courses, and I pass the GED exam on the 1st try. I recall that the passing score is 225, and that I score 297 — even though I'm not a native speaker of English.

Now that I have a GED, I wonder what my next step should be. One night at an NA meeting, I share that I want to go to college, but I'm unsure where to apply. After the meeting, a woman comes up to me and says, "I work at Kingston College in their Adult Curriculum Education [ACE] department. ACE is an accelerated program that's geared toward adults, 25 or older, who work and are just entering college. It might be a good place for you to start. And, some courses are 6 credits, so those will help you build up credits faster."

This sounds good. I apply for the ACE program, and take their entrance test in reading, writing, and math. I do fine in reading and writing, passing those tests the 1st time.

But I flunk the math test twice. After failing the 2nd time, I get very worried. I don't want to fail a 3rd time. So for about 2 months, I go twice a week to Kingston College's math lab, and teach myself basic algebra plus some geometry (which I was exposed to in the 9th grade in Italy, but never really "got"). Now that I've taught myself enough algebra and geometry, I pass the math section on the 3rd try.

At last, I'm accepted to Kingston College. My classes get underway in the fall of 1990, just as I'm turning 32. By now, I'm working for Magda, so I can also afford tuition, books, fees, and a babysitter to watch my sons while I'm at school. Carol, my new housemate, also helps financially.

(After Carlos goes into rehab and can no longer help out, but before starting to work at Magda's, I put ads in the local laundromat looking for a roommate. Carol responds. She's been living in her car, after escaping from an abusive relationship. Even though she has a regular job, she can't afford to pay a month's advance rent plus 2 months' deposit, which is what's required to move into an apartment in NYC. So, she's grateful to move in with me.)

I give Carol the master bedroom, which has its own bathroom. My sons get the other bedroom, and I sleep in the dining area. It doesn't have a door, but that doesn't matter, because I don't have a boyfriend anymore.

I hire a babysitter for the daytime, but on nights when I have a class, or classes, it helps that Carol is at home. Hiring and keeping a babysitter is always complicated, because 2 active boys can be a challenge. Fortunately, as I'm writing this, they're now fine young men. Both have a BA. One has married a lovely girl, and they have a young son. The other is engaged to another nice girl. But, back then, the 2 of them combined could be a lot to handle.

It's all constant stress for me, so I start out taking 3 classes, unsure if I can handle more. I do surprisingly well — it's a really good experience!

So, maybe there *is* hope that I can escape the cycle of poverty my lack of education has kept me and my boys trapped in. Maybe working for Magda will turn out to be more than just an emergency exit from imminent homelessness.

A Small Price to Pay

As things turn out, I *can* do it all without a man in my life. I'm able to juggle working at Magda's while raising my boys, plus get good grades at college-level coursework. I do it by shutting down a part of myself that needed to be put in storage anyway: dating men. I become like a hawk zeroing in on the prize — getting a bachelor's degree to make a better life for myself and my sons.

During the 4½ years it takes me to graduate from Kingston, I work at Magda's, then Ally's, and lastly Angela's. As noted, I try to minimize inner emotional conflict by looking at the work as a sociological field project. I study the girls, the clients, and the whatever that goes on, all the while trying to integrate it with what I'm learning in school.

As mentioned already, when I was a child I had to endure sleeping in bed beside father, from the time mother left til I was 13. He didn't touch me, but sometimes when he was drunk, he touched himself lying there next to me. And, during this time in my life, I had to sit with him in our sauna for lengthy periods — with both of us in the nude. While driving the car, he'd put his hand on my thigh as if I were his lover. I wasn't allowed to say, *Don't do this!*

So, after everything I went through with father for years, it's a piece of cake to spend a few minutes of physical intimacy with one of my regular clients. Those few minutes are a small price to pay, because they allow me to resume my formal education, while keeping my sons happy and healthy.

I've been guilt-ridden for messing up my life, and my son's, by squandering on drugs all that father worked for his whole life. Now I feel an overwhelming need to accomplish something constructive. I can't live with myself otherwise.

Further, my academic goals keep me from seeking out romance. I'm grateful for this, because I realize I'm not yet healthy enough to find the right man. So I barely date at all. I have a few platonic friendships, but nothing serious.

The Only One

My grades are mainly A's (sometimes an A- or B+). Throughout my time as an undergraduate, I get only one C, which I receive in a course on child psychology.

I get the C because I've been working very late 1 or 2 nights a week at Ally's, and this child psychology class begins at 8 AM. On some nights, I get home at 3 AM or 4 AM. To arrive in class by 8 AM, I have to bring Johan to the babysitter by 6:30 AM. Then she takes him to school when it opens. A little later, Lukas walks by himself from home to school.

One morning I get to class exhausted, because I worked really late the night before. It turns out we're having a mid-term exam — *Damn, I completely forgot about it!*

As it is, I'm often half asleep in this class. Plus, I find the teacher is too focused on her own specialty, childhood autism. Other areas of child psychology (such as abandonment by one parent and abusive parenting by the other, as in my childhood) are touched upon only superficially.

So, I'm not prepared at all for the mid-term. Fortunately, I'm friends with Emiliana. She's super smart, and we sit next to each other (in a lecture hall that seems large enough to be a stadium). I say to her, "Unless I see some of your answers, I'm going to completely fail this course."

I'm terrified of getting caught cheating. But, I manage to avoid detection. As things turns out, due to Emiliana letting me look at her work, I get some of the answers right. (This is the only time I ever cheated in school.)

Although I get a D+ on the midterm, I get a B+ on the final exam (for which I've prepared in earnest). My overall grade is C, which, as noted, is the lowest grade I get as a Kingston College undergraduate.

Course of Study

For a long time while at Kingston, I struggle with deciding what to major in. I've always been athletic, and I really like physical education courses, so I consider becoming a physical education teacher.

I also think about majoring in nutrition, because I've had a lifelong interest in healthy eating.

And yet, I want to study art too. I take classes in drawing, painting, and sculpture — and do well in all 3.

However, my interest always returns to psychology. I think to myself, *If I major in psychology, I can still take art classes and physical education classes as electives.*

In the end, I do major in psychology.

As a psych major, I have to study statistics. Initially it's like a foreign language to me. As with studying math on my own to get into Kingston's ACE program, I get extra books and tutor myself. Statistics seem so weird at first. For about 6 weeks, I don't understand anything. Suddenly (as with learning a new language), it clicks and all makes sense.

The whole process is amazing. I realize that I do have a brain that functions, and that I'm able to learn all this new information. I end up getting a B+ in statistics. I'm pretty happy about this, because I messed up the first 2 tests. But after tutoring myself, I get in the 90's, sometimes 100, on my remaining tests.

I Still Almost Don't Finish

I'd have graduated in 4 years, but I'm preoccupied with personal concerns after mother dies in a plane crash in January 1994. So, I fail to register in time for a required course in experimental psychology.

Even when fall rolls around, I almost don't sign up for this class. Marco is now in the picture, so I've been under that much more stress. As detailed above, I'm very upset that I've allowed him in my life at all, never mind in my home.

I'm still friends with Tracie, the girl I went with to the NA convention where I met Marco. She was also with me when I encountered him a 2nd time, at the sober swim-and-dance party. Now she's *Marco's* friend too. In fact, she comes to my house and sits with him — while they eat *my* food. (The 2 of them are very chummy together.)

With all of this happening under my roof, by the last day to enroll for the fall 1994 semester, I still haven't registered for that final required class. Marco, who all along has felt threatened by my improving myself, says, "Don't worry about it — you'll take the class next year."

Yet, something inside of me says, *If I don't register to take this class now, I will never graduate. I'm in a terrible relationship with an abusive guy who doesn't want me to get ahead, so he's trying to keep me under his thumb. But, I've worked too hard to not finish.*

This last class, experimental psychology, turns out to be very difficult for me. I feel as if every hair on my body wants to give up. But, I push through.

In the end, I graduate with a 3.5 GPA — *summa cum laude*. I'm pretty excited about it!

But I still have this loser living with me, and I don't know how to get rid of him. I almost didn't finish school, partly because being stuck with him was so depressing.

Grad School

Although I now have a BA in psychology, I'm not sure if I'm capable of helping other people with *their* emotional turmoil, because I'm still in the midst of *my own*. Plus, working with abused children can lead to burnout. I feel I might be better suited for working in an administrative role at a social service agency.

And so, that fall I enroll in a program at Gramercy University in Manhattan to get a Master's degree in Public Administration. My classes are 1 or 2 nights during the work week, and just about all day Saturday. This is in addition to my working 9-to-5 Monday to Friday at Manhattan Family Hospital, a job my BA in psychology has enabled me to get.

The good news is that I'm hardly ever home with Marco. As noted, at night I study until he falls asleep, so I can avoid his touch. That alone is a big motivation to study, a way to carve out some time for myself and keep him at a distance.

The bad part is that my sons also rarely see me. I feel a lot of remorse for bringing this monster into their life, having his children imposing on them, and my no longer having enough money for the household.

As mentioned, we were much better off before Marco came into the picture. When I was working for Angela, I had more time for my sons, and we had a higher living standard — win-win.

I've never cared about having lots of outfits, or Gucci bags, or Prada shoes, or getting my nails perfectly done, etc. I've always been more the hippie type. And, I'd stopped all drug abuse years earlier. So, by working at Angela's 1 or 2 nights a week to supplement my starting wage at Manhattan Family, though my sons and I lived modestly, we were still comfortable.

But, once Marco wouldn't let me work at Angela's, what little he brought into the household (when rain didn't discourage him from going to work at all), failed to cover even my loss of income from Angela's, much less the added expense of him and his teenage son and daughter.

So during my time at Gramercy U, my boys and I are back on the edge of poverty, always pinched financially. This economic insecurity adds greatly to the stress I'm under from everything else. I feel I've messed up my life, *again*.

In spite of all the turmoil, in May 1997 I receive my Master's degree in Public Administration from Gramercy University. I graduate at the top of the class, with a perfect 4.0 GPA. Because of this, I receive a $5,000 grant that's applied to my student-loan indebtedness.

A 2nd Master's Degree

To review: About a month after I graduate from Gramercy U, Marco goes berserk one night (perhaps partly due to the widening gap in our status) and assaults Johan. This time he's gone too far. I have the police remove him from our house, once and for all.

But because Marco's life is so unstable, and his teenagers are already under my roof, I tell them they can stay until they finish high school. Now that I have a Master's degree, Manhattan Family raises my pay to $27,000/yr. Since I have 4 teens to feed, $27,000 won't cut it. I'm soon back working at Angela's. At last, I can breathe again financially.

By this point, I've gained confidence that I can be a psychotherapist after all. In fall 1997, on the strength of my academic record at Kingston College and Gramercy U, I'm accepted to prestigious Uptown University's Graduate School of Social Work.

To my surprise, I'm disappointed by the program at Uptown University. In particular, I'm underwhelmed by a number of my professors. But, I do learn a lot from a few of them. For example, there's Marvin. An older man with a pacemaker and huge feet, Marvin looks a bit like Uncle Fester from the *Addams Family* television show. Yet, Marvin's very intelligent, and he's been tenured at Uptown University forever.

In class, he'd sing what he says was his high school's anthem:

> *If you want to get rich,*
> *You son of a bitch,*
> *I'll tell you what to do:*
> *Never sit down with a smile or a frown,*
> *and paddle your own canoe.*

I've never forgotten this advice.

Marvin teaches us Chaos Theory, how it applies to social service agencies generally, and especially to agencies in NYC. In essence, it's the study of how the smallest events can have enormous unexpected consequences later on. Marvin's an interesting guy all around.

Letitia, my Master's thesis supervisor (I mentioned earlier she was harassed by her ex), is another excellent professor. She teaches a seminar with only 8 students. I'm in her seminar for a year, and it's probably the best experience I have at Uptown University.

I also take a class on drug and alcohol issues. The professor is very good, but the course contains nothing I don't already know from my undergraduate work as a psychology major at Kingston College (plus my personal experiences).

And, there's a course on Ego Psychology that I find really thought-provoking. But, otherwise, I don't find the overall program at Uptown University worthwhile. There are a lot of public policy classes (thus, non-clinical), and a research class (likewise, non-clinical) that's a waste of time, because it's much too easy. I'm not challenged, so I'm bored a lot of the time.

Overall, I feel let down by Uptown University. In spite of its prestige, I learned a lot more at Kingston College and Gramercy University. Given the tuition Uptown charges, I don't think it offers nearly as much educational value as the other 2. But I know that having a Master's degree from Uptown will open doors for me.

And so, after 3 years of hard work, in 2001 I receive my 2nd Master's degree, this one in Clinical Social Work. (During this period, I was working for Angela from June of 1997 to sometime in 2000.)

In total, I attend school in America for 10 years in order to obtain a GED, a Bachelor's degree, and 2 Master's degrees, while working and raising 2 sons mainly on my own.

Hal: A Son of the Holocaust

By 2000, Marco's daughter is married, and his son is still in the Marines. My younger son, Johan, graduates from high school, and my older son, Lukas, moves in with his girl-friend. In the fall, Johan goes off to college.

Since Marco's children moved on, my sons and I have been living in a rental apartment attached to a residential home. But now the owner is selling the house, and the new owner wants all of it for his own family. I have to look for another place, and I know I don't want it to be in Astoria, because Marco still lives there.

Detail from my apartment in Astoria.

That same summer, Hal and I meet at a local NA group. Over time, we get to know each other better. I'd share at meetings about the ordeal I've been going through with Marco. And Hal would share about his troubled upbringing and adult life. After my experience with Marco's malevo-lence, it's a relief to find someone like Hal — a really good man who feels very safe to be with.

Hal becomes an important person in my life for the next 2 or 3 years. He's smart, funny, and he speaks some German.

Not much, but that little bit is another reason I enjoy his company. Hal and I start getting closer, and we date a few times. It isn't really a boyfriend/girlfriend type of relationship (for me, at least). It's more of a warm friendship.

Meanwhile, in spite of the order of protection, Marco continues to stalk me. He notices my hanging out with Hal, and learns the location of the basement apartment Hal lives in.

Around the same time, someone just happens to call the Building Department about it, and an inspector comes out to investigate. The family who own the house are really kind people who've been renting their basement to Hal at an affordable price. However, the apartment doesn't meet the Building Department's (countless) requirements, so this family is now in a lot of trouble. Hal and I strongly suspect that Marco is the one who called, because he's so spiteful by nature.

I feel very guilty about Hal and this family being in trouble because of my connection to Marco. So I suggest to Hal, "Since we already get along, why don't we get an apartment together? We can share expenses, and see how things go."

Hal agrees. So in January 2001, I rent a 2-bedroom place in Rego Park, Queens, and Hal moves in with me. We each have our own bedroom, while sharing a small living room and a kitchen. I have 2 cats, and he has 1. It kind of works.

Hal's Backstory

As we get to know each other better, Hal shares more of his life story. Both his parents were from northern Germany. Hal's father, Oskar, was from a wealthy family that had land they raised horses on. Oskar was getting work, and starting to be noticed, as an actor and playwright. Hal's mother, Helen, was working as a nurse.

When Hitler comes to power, though, Hal's parents are suddenly in a perilous situation. They're able to find refuge in Shanghai, China, which has had an established Jewish community since the 1840's. However, they can't take their financial assets with them; just some personal effects like clothing.

Throughout World War II, Shanghai is occupied by Japan. Though allied with Germany, Japan doesn't share Hitler's murderous designs on Jews. In 1946, a year after its liberation from Japan, Hal is born in Shanghai. But in 1949, after a protracted civil war, a Communist government under Mao Zedong comes to power. Because of a century of colonial interference in China's affairs, Mao has virtually all non-Chinese people expelled from the country.

However, the modern state of Israel has recently declared its independence, so Hal's parents emigrate there. At the time, Israel is not yet economically developed. Hal remembers being very poor as a young child. He and his family live in a refugee camp. Their hut has a dirt floor. However, Hal also recalls having a lot of fun there. He has many friends, and they climb hills and run around in a natural setting.

Hal's parents plant a vegetable garden, and make big salads with cucumbers, tomatoes, parsley, and other vegetables, all cut into tiny bits. (Hal makes similar salads for the 2 of us.)

When Hal is 10, his parents win Israel's national lottery. With the winnings, they relocate again, this time to Maspeth, Queens, where relatives of theirs are already living. (Hal is still living in Maspeth when we meet.)

So, Hal's parents were transplanted from Germany to China to Israel to the US. They didn't learn Chinese, and didn't really learn Hebrew. Helen, though, seems to have adjusted better along the way. Oskar hasn't adjusted well at all.

Now in the US, they're starting from scratch again. Over time, Helen gets recredentialed and back into nursing. But Oskar is unable to get a substantial job. He's a miserable man, and an angry one. He never wanted to leave Germany, where he felt he had a bright future. And, he doesn't like the United States, where he feels thwarted at every turn. He's resentful about everything that's happened to him.

Sadly, Hal's life has been indelibly scarred by 2nd generation Holocaust trauma. As a result of Oskar's bitterness about his own life, he's very abusive to Hal. For example, he'd hit Hal and tell him he's worthless. Helen tries to protect Hal, but there's only so much she can do.

By the time Hal is 12, he's already getting into trouble, making the wrong friends, acting out in school, getting poor grades, and eventually using drugs and alcohol.

In the mid-1960's, Hal leaves home, drops out of school, and moves to Greenwich Village in downtown Manhattan. This is the era of "Turn on. Tune in. Drop out." Hal plugs into this scene, and becomes increasingly estranged from his family. Oskar wants nothing to do with him. Helen pleads with Hal to get his life back on track. But, by the time he's in his 20's, Hal is heavily addicted to cocaine.

In what at first seems like a hopeful sign, he gets married. The couple have 2 boys: Hal, Jr. and Keith. But due to his addiction, Hal isn't able to be a responsible husband and father. Eventually he's arrested on drug-related charges and spends 3 years in prison. (In broad outline, this parallels my relationship with Fabio, the father of *my* 2 sons.)

A lifetime of setbacks and disappointments has hardened Oskar. He sees Hal's imprisonment as the final proof that Hal is no good. So Hal doesn't get any emotional support from him.

The years go by. Hal ends up homeless, sleeping in hallways. (His nickname in NA is "Hallway Hal".) He loses touch with his sons. By the time I meet him, his older son, Hal, Jr., is married and has 3 children. His younger son, Keith, is having his own issues with drugs.

Although Hal is very smart, because of what was done to him while growing up, plus his own acting out, he's never been able to realize his full potential. He has a job working in a supermarket. The job barely pays enough for him to afford his basement apartment in Maspeth, and even then only because its illegal status keeps the rent low. Fortunately, Hal has the survival skills to really stretch a dollar.

Undocumented

As I get to know him better, I learn he has no identity papers, because he lost everything while he was homeless. Since he didn't know how to get real papers, he's been working under someone else's Social Security number.

According to Hal, when he was born China wasn't issuing birth certificates for newborn children of foreign parents. Unfortunately, a birth certificate is required for getting other forms of US identification. Based upon what I've learned as an immigrant myself, I say to Hal, "I'll help you make an FOIA (Freedom of Information Act) request. The INS has to have a record of you and your parents."

I help him with filling out and mailing in the FOIA forms. After 2 or 3 months, a big envelope from the INS arrives in our mailbox. Hal opens it, and finds it has *everything*. By this time (the early 2000's), both his parents have been dead for a number of years. But, Hal now has Oskar's birth certificate, Helen's birth certificate, and their marriage certificate. He learns the exact day his family arrived in America, and he even learns that Oskar was married before his marriage to Helen. Most importantly, Hal at last has an official birth certificate, *plus* documentation that he's a naturalized citizen.

After 15 years without papers, Hal is finally able to work using his real name, and to make payments to Social Security into an account that he'll someday be able to draw on.

The *What If's?*

Who knows how Oskar and Helen's lives would've turned out if they hadn't been forced to flee Nazi Germany? Hal's father might have had a fulfilling life as an actor and playwright. Hal's mother might have risen higher in the medical profession. (On the other hand, Hal might not have been born had his parents not fled to China at the time.)

Many tens of millions of people around the world died, or had a life that was permanently diminished, because of World War II, as well as related events before and long after. In Hal's case, as a child of German Jews, who himself is born in China, spends his early years in Israel, and then comes to the US at age 10, he's never felt he had a permanent home.

This is common among people forced by fate to immigrate. In my case, it's hard for me to relate to New York as my real home. I never feel as connected here as I did in South Tyrol. Sunlit fields look a different shade of green. Trees and grass don't smell the same. When I wake up in the morning, the air itself seems different. *Everything* is different.

I've had no choice but to let go of a lot of things. On the upside, I now can adapt to living anywhere. Still, a part of me would feel more at home in my hometown, Bolzitano, or my birthplace, Berlin, than in NYC. It's a bittersweet feeling.

It's similar for Hal. New York has become his home, but he still misses Israel. He misses the garden they had there, and walking around barefoot. For his parents, particularly his father, leaving Germany was traumatic. Emigration, especially under desperate circumstances, profoundly changes a person. It alters both their inner and outer landscape forever. Sadly, Oskar's trauma was passed on to Hal.

More research needs to be done on children of Holocaust survivors. But my impression, based in part upon subsequent clinical experience (discussed below), is that sometimes the 1st generation survivors, because of their own trauma, are unable to meet the needs of their children. This may result in their children engaging in various kinds of self-defeating patterns.

Sharing My Story With Hal

In turn, I'd share with Hal about my parents. Our backgrounds are in some ways similar. His parents were both German; mine were German and Austrian. Both his father and mine were permanently damaged by World War II. Obviously, his father and my father were in completely different circumstances. Yet, I think that people who've been traumatized by war still have some things in common.

It's understandable that most readers won't have any sympathy for my father. After all, he was a Nazi who never repented. But, other readers may take into account that the hysterical nationalism of the era was a global phenomenon that swept up a lot of people who were much older and had more reason to know better. Father had just turned 20 when he left home for the 1st time — to fight in WW II. For the next 5½ years (3 of them spent on the Russian front), he saw unparalleled death, disfigurement, and destruction all around him, including to many of those closest to him at that time. This has to leave deep emotional scars on any young adult — even a Nazi.

Whatever the difference in the specifics of their trauma, neither Hal's father nor mine was available for emotional support when we were growing up. I feel it's more than coincidence that Hal and I acted out in similar ways.

But eventually, I caught up to my peers by getting more education and becoming a psychotherapist. Hal hasn't been as fortunate. Many people who fall behind in life don't fully recover lost ground.

Ironically, though father was instrumental in my downfall, I feel my eventual recovery is also due to his influence. I inherited his drive and entrepreneurial knack, for which I'm grateful. I often talk to father in my imagination. I ask him if he's proud of me. Because, sometimes when he was angry, he'd tell me that I would never amount to anything. Similarly, Hal's father would say to him, *Du bist ein stück dreck.* ("You're a piece of dirt.") What parent says such a thing — unless the parent is very damaged?

Oskar often talked about the play he wrote while still in Germany. Audiences loved it. The applause went on and on. Looking back, he'd say, "If we'd stayed in Germany, I'd have been famous." Oskar never got over it. He was a broken man. Hal (like me) is an only child. Whenever Oskar was in a bad mood, Hal was the only convenient scapegoat.

Now that he's an adult, Hal understands this. But a child tends to believe a parent. He doesn't know how to say to himself, *My father has been traumatized, so this isn't really about me. He's miserable himself, and feels like he's a loser. So he's projecting all of this onto me.*

Social Media

As mentioned, after getting the police to remove Marco from my house in 1997, I return to working at Angela's. But, in 2000, I get my own escorting website. Everything is different now that I'm running my own business. No more traveling back and forth to a workplace — whether I'll have a client or not. No more shifts with fixed starting and stopping times. No more having to sit around hoping a client would appear. I'm now my own boss (more details below).

Hal knows about my website. He's one of the most open-minded and tolerant people I've ever known, and he always looks out for me. Sometimes when I go to meet a client, I call Hal and tell him when I've arrived. And, I call him again when I'm returning, so he knows I'm okay.

Because I'm a "webscort", on top of my day job at Manhattan Family Hospital, I make more money than Hal. So I cover most of our expenses. Hal does pay part of the rent, but I pay most of it, plus everything else. But, he'd make dinner for me, and afterward we'd watch a movie. It's a pretty peaceful time in my life — a great relief after living with Marco.

Caretaker in Chief

Hal and I live together for about a year and a half. But eventually I have to leave, because he's becoming too dependent on me. Hal still has unresolved issues, including what appears to be post-traumatic stress disorder. He sometimes has anxiety attacks, and even severe panic attacks. In short, he's very emotionally needy.

Unfortunately, he also falls in love with me, and that's not the relationship I want with him. It's hard for me to go, because I want him to be okay, and I worry about him. He's very emotionally vulnerable, so he's hurt that I'm leaving. But I care for Hal as a friend, not a lover.

I have a tendency to be a caretaker for other people. I was father's caretaker from an early age, so I've long been familiar with this role. I'm pretty good at it, but there's a price to be paid for this. I often put the other person's needs ahead of mine.

And so, I feel I must leave Hal. He'll be back to having to survive on his own, which has always been a challenge for him. He worries he won't be able to pay the rent without help. Understandably, he's upset (and maybe a bit resentful). I gently explain he must get a roommate. The day I leave and move into my own apartment, we both feel sad.

Hoping to become a drug counselor, Hal returns to school for about a year. But it's too hard for him. It may be that he did drugs for too long to still be able to concentrate on academic work. I don't think he finishes the program.

A Sad Existence

Recently, Hal calls me on the telephone (after a hiatus of almost a decade). I've always had a special place in my heart for Hal, so I'm happy to hear from him. In AA and NA, and 12-step programs generally, stories are shared by a lot of people who've gone through tremendous trials and tribulations. But Hal was the one person I could especially identify with. He was an important part of my life for the 2 or 3 years that we were close friends.

Hal tells me he's doing okay. He's now retired and living on Social Security. He's making a life for himself, to the extent that he can. But, it's a sad existence.

Since he gets little monthly income (especially relative to the high cost of living in New York), he's living modestly somewhere in the Bronx. Keith, the son with a drug problem of his own, committed suicide by hanging himself. His older son, Hal, Jr., is still deeply resentful that Hal wasn't available when he was growing up, and he now wants nothing to do with him. He won't even allow Hal to see his grandchildren.

𝕭ebscort

Going Indie

Returning to the mid-1997 timeframe: As discussed above, after the police remove Marco from my home in Astoria, I resume working at Angela's, in addition to my day job at Manhattan Family. Angela, as also mentioned, is a really sexy woman who works out at the gym everyday, and is very savvy about money. She and her husband are steadily accumulating real estate with her earnings.

(Magda is now out of the picture. She accused Angela of stealing her half of the business. So, now they aren't talking to each other.)

At this time, Angela's place is on West 47th Street, in the heart of NYC's Diamond District, with its heavy foot traffic (and landlords who don't ask many questions).

By 2000, though, Magda has her own place again, and I'm back working for her. I'm not the most popular escort there. After all, I'm now twice the age of some of the girls (and none of them are minors). But though I'm not the prettiest or sexiest, I still do well, by using my schooling in psychology and social work, and my genuine interest in helping people with unmet needs. In spite of the well known male desire for variety, a number of men become my regulars.

It's during this period that I make friends with Tara and Debbie, who also work at Magda's. Tara doesn't do too well. She herself once said, "I was never a good ho." Debbie does not do very well either. A lot of men think she's too skinny. (Debbie *is* slim, but I think she's very pretty.)

Magda's daughter, Nicole, is also an escort. Some of us can recall her visits to the 2nd Avenue location. Back then, Magda would pretend Nicole doesn't know what's going on. She'd say, "Don't talk about clients. My daughter is coming over, and she thinks this is a straight massage parlor." We'd think, *Yeah, right.* Regardless, Nicole still winds up in the business (though Magda never mentions it).

(Readers of Book I may recall that my new car was totaled while I was stopped at a traffic light on my way home from seeing *Phantom of the Opera*. Not mentioned was that I went to the show at the invitation of Magda and Nicole.)

In the late 1990's, escorts start to advertise adult services on websites. This soon becomes "a thing". It happens that Nicole is the 1st girl I know to have her own website, probably in 1999. Another girl at Magda's gets a website too.

Then Tara leaves Magda's. Soon, she calls me and says, "Marlena, you don't have to work at Magda's anymore. Having a website is much better. You'll run your own business, and instead of splitting the fee with Magda or Angela, you'll get to keep it all. I'll show you how."

I visit Tara's sunny apartment, located in a lovely Brooklyn neighborhood. She takes a few pictures of me. The picture I use on my website shows just my back above the waist.

Tara also comes up with my screen name. We sit around one afternoon wondering what it should be. Tara says, "You have naturally blonde hair, blue eyes, a German accent, and you were born in Berlin — just like Marlene Dietrich. Why not use the name "Marlene" on your website?" To be a little different, I choose "Marlena" as my screen name.

Tara connects me with Stamford Stan, a client of her own. Stan's pretty old, surely in his 70's. Though he has lots of money, he rents a really cheap motel room in Stamford for his encounters with escorts. Still, it's my start as an "indie".

Tara, Debbie, and I have a buddy system. (Sometimes we even exchange clients.) For safety's sake, when one of us has an appointment, she calls one of the others to say where she's going and how long she expects to be there. Then calls again when she arrives, and calls as soon as she leaves. (Sometimes Tara and Debbie aren't available. That's when I call Hal instead.)

I start to do well with my website, and become pretty popular on certain escorting-related message boards. I leave Magda's, and stop working at Manhattan Family. My website allows me to stay focused on getting a Master's degree from Uptown University, including having time for my 3-day a week psychotherapy internship.

Graduation Day

Hal is there to see me receive my diploma, when I graduate from Uptown U in May 2001. But, I'm still not sure I want to continue doing clinical social work. I've spent years working with physically and sexually abused children in foster care. There are many cases of horrendous child abuse in NYC (and everywhere else), and it's hard for any therapist to avoid emotional burnout.

I choose an Employee Assistance Program (EAP) for my internship. The program provides short-term treatment — only 3 to 6 sessions. But, it's solid experience for me, because I get to help a range of people who are hurting, from fire fighters to investment bankers. I learn a lot during this year, both in the EAP and from my appointments as a webscort (things that aren't taught in school).

Hearing From The Dean

One of the funny things that happens while I'm a student at Uptown U is that the Dean of the Social Work School contacts me through my escorting website, wanting to set up a session. Naturally, he'll be the one handing out the diplomas at the commencement ceremony when I graduate!

Luckily, in response to my pre-screening email, he provides his real name (not all men do), and says he works as the dean of a university (though he doesn't specify which one). But, I recognize his name as the dean at my school. I think to myself, *Omigod, how embarrassing my graduation ceremony would've been for both of us if he hadn't been honest about his name and job!* Little does this dean realize that his school has formally trained me to approach adult companionship as a special type of social work.

Right of Privacy

Of course, I don't set up a session with him. Still, it's an example of the many interesting people — on both ends of the pillow — that I meet in this business. But also, the diffe-rence between what women and men do in public, and what they do behind closed doors.

I find this duality fascinating. Beneath the surface, many of us have urges that, though harmless in themselves, are too at odds with social norms to act out, or even talk about, in public. Yet, these urges often are acted out in private.

For that reason, I feel it's a privilege to work as an escort. To know people in a much more candid way, without their social disguise, without so much conventionality.

For example, there are men who like to wear women's inti-mate wear beneath their Wall Street business attire. They're hurting no one, but it's "too much information" to let co-workers know about — not to mention the wife at home.

This illuminates a double standard. Society's gender stric-tures are more flexible for women. Women can wear cloth-ing similar to men's, for instance a pantsuit. But, if a man wears a skirt, he's ridiculed. He's labeled "queer" or "weird".

I think women have it easier that way. If a man occasionally indulges in wearing pantyhose or a pink teddy, he's going to lose status as a man if others find out. And his significant other may leave him if she learns of it. I come across this issue often. In a non-threatening and non-judgmental way, I've helped these men to accept and enjoy themselves, and then go back to their "normal" life and carry on as before.

First as an adult-companion, and later as a psychothera-pist, seeing how vulnerable so many *other* people are helps me accept *myself.* Many of us are too hard on ourselves. We hide things we feel are shameful and wrong (even though we aren't hurting anyone) because we fear that enjoying these things means we are abnormal.

And yet, many times I've been in a 4- or 5-star hotel with a man who just wants a human touch from someone who doesn't judge him for some little quirk. Someone who can help him relax and feel good about himself. That's what much of adult-companionship often comes down to, at least at the high end.

Sometimes a client I've gotten from my website has traveled to New York on business. He might fly in for 1 night for a meeting the next day, or a few days for a convention. In either case, though there are millions of people in this big city, he's all alone. What he wants, and needs, is a woman's touch, rather than having to spend his evening all alone.

My typical client is a nice, respectful gentleman. He might treat me to an expensive meal with champagne or other fine wine. He might bring a present — chocolate, perfume, jewelry — all kinds of things. He customarily treats escorts better than many boyfriends treat the woman in their life — certainly much better than every man I was romantically involved with. In many ways, it's an amazing experience.

And, of course, the hourly pay is much better than what I was making in retailing, real estate, or social work. As when I worked for Magda, and later Ally and Angela, I'm not trying to maximize financial gain as a webscort. I have no interest in expensive clothing, shoes, handbags, etc. I drive around in an old car that I bought used. I live in a small rented home in a modest working-class neighborhood. My goal all along has been to make ends meet, and maximize the time available to spend with my sons, pay for my own schooling, and later help my sons pay for their college education. So, it's not about acquiring material possessions. It's about changing my life — and that of my sons.

I'm well aware that many girls have been very damaged by the business. But, like everything else in life, not everyone's experience is the same. For me, things worked out well.

More Than Money

Further, there have been benefits beyond reaching my financial goals. For example, getting to know Mel. As described above, he's about 400 pounds when he first becomes my client. He eventually sends me a letter expressing his gratitude, because I inspired him to lose a lot of that weight. I find his letter very emotionally rewarding.

A number of former clients have become social friends, and we've stayed in touch. My 1st date with Guy, a writer and photographer, takes place in the late summer of 2001, just a few weeks before 9/11. I'm always a little uneasy when meeting a first-time client. So we rendezvous at an outdoor café on Manhattan's Upper West Side. Debbie has a nearby apartment that she's letting me use. We sit at the café waiting for Guy to show up. (She's my backup, in case he gives off a bad vibe and I want to call off the date.)

Guy arrives wearing charcoal-gray flannel slacks, a blue Oxford shirt with a button-down collar, and retro Ray Ban sunglasses. He's short, middle-aged, and has a paunch — absolutely no sex appeal. He's carrying a black gym bag, but instead of a change of workout clothing, his bag contains a 35mm camera, lenses, and other photo gear.

As a gift, Guy presents me with a CD of a special pan-European performance of Beethoven's Choral Symphony (conducted by the Bronx's own Leonard Bernstein) to celebrate the tearing down of the Berlin Wall, which had divided the city of my birth since the early 1960's.

At the time, Guy seems a bit odd to me. (He still does.) But, he also seems harmless. So, I discreetly signal Debbie that I consider the situation safe enough for her to leave, which she soon does. In the years since then, Guy has photographed — without asking anything in return — a wedding of 2 dear friends, plus the wedding of my sister, and that of a cousin from South Tyrol whose love of New York brought the couple here for their nuptials.

Warning Signs

However, not all clients are as harmless as Guy. So, I'm always cautious before agreeing to meet a new one. For example, I call back the phone number he has given me, to make sure that he answers — and therefore is traceable.

Even so, one new client whips out a silk scarf and wraps it around my neck! He says he's into "erotic asphyxiation". I'm *not*. So naturally I put a stop to it right away.

There's another incident with a pretty scary client. I join him at a restaurant in Westchester County (which sits on the northern border of the Bronx). I don't first call the hotel that he says he's staying in. Instead I think to myself, *Let me meet him first.*

He turns out to be a really good looking man. But my gut instinct tells me that something isn't right. Earlier over the phone, he told me he's a veterinarian, and that he's in Westchester to attend a veterinary conference. But, when I asked for his name and where his veterinary practice is located, he didn't want to tell me.

Once we sit down to dinner, he continues making me feel uncomfortable. I try to break the ice with chit-chat, but he barely responds. His whole vibe feels weird and creepy. I ask him about various things — nothing personal, just general stuff — but he's evasive about *everything.*

After a bit he says, "You ask a lot of questions."

I reply, "Well I'm trying to make conversation."

He follows up, "I like to fly under the radar."

I'm thinking, *If you want to fly under the radar, that's okay. But, I'm not sure I want to fly with you.*

When I've gotten the sense he has been lying about *a lot* of things, I excuse myself to go to the restroom. But on the way, I call the hotel he said he's staying in, and ask them to ring his room. The hotel desk tells me that no one is listed there under the name he gave me.

I think he realizes I've figured him out, because when I return to our table, he's left the restaurant. Now I'm afraid he's dangerous. Since I don't know if he's lurking about, I ask the restaurant manager to accompany me to my car.

Although he may be a married guy using a fake name just to be sure his wife never finds out about our date, his whole vibe scared me. He's one of my last clients as an escort. I've gained enough confidence in myself as a psychotherapist that I soon stop escorting entirely.

Afterthought

The rare scary client notwithstanding, the experience of a typical middle class adult-companion, such as myself and my friends Tara, Debbie, and Angela, isn't the horror story that the media typically portray. Sure, we wouldn't be doing this work if we weren't getting paid. And, there are times we wish we were in some other line of work.

But, just as surely, lots of people feel that way about whatever job they have. I certainly had those feelings about many of my other jobs — plus they paid very poorly.

In fact, about 6 months after quitting the business, I got a little wistful about the excitement and good times I was no longer having. And, some girls do go back after leaving — because they have no better alternative. But, I now have the education and work experience to move on in life. Fortunately, I didn't wait until I reached an age where I had to quit, without having prepared for the next stage of my life.

A final observation: Many women dress up as trashy street-walkers for Halloween, indulging a fantasy they must find attractive at some level. But when they think about people who actually *are* sex workers, the very same women tend to view this work as something really awful to actually experience.

Again, it's part of life's inevitable duality.

Yoga Training

In the fall of 2001 Johan's still in college, and Lukas continues to live at his girlfriend's. There's only Hal at home. I've saved enough money to pay my fixed expenses for the next 2 months (in stark contrast to my life before Magda's). So, as a break from social work, a little after 9/11 Tara and I sign up for a 9-week training program in Los Angeles for teaching Bikram Chadhury ("hot yoga").

We travel to the West Coast in Tara's old car, an adventure in itself — especially when the car breaks down in the Mojave Desert!

Hoping to cover our travel expenses, we post on an online escort/client message board that we'll be visiting LA and available for appointments once there. As things turn out, we don't get much work. I have maybe 3 appointments, and Tara has perhaps 2. But, escort work isn't why we're there. We're there to learn to be yoga teachers.

We get back to New York in December 2001. Now that I'm out of grad school, I'm able to practice psychotherapy full-time. A social worker friend calls to tell me that many New Yorkers need help dealing with their trauma from 9/11. She asks if I want to work for SWU 75, the service-workers union, in their Employee Assistance Program. I'd be paid. (It's not an internship). I say to myself, *It's a start.*

I start working for SWU 75 in early 2002, at their main office in downtown Manhattan. The job lasts the better part of a year, until I'm let go when they decide to outsource their EAP. But while working for SWU 75, I'm also slowly building up my own psychotherapy practice on the side.

My goal all along has been to transition into a professional career. Yet now that I have psychotherapy clients, plus having been trained as a Yoga instructor (while still doing a little escorting with a few long-term clients), I'm left wondering: *Which road(s) should I stay on?*

Should I enlarge my psychotherapy practice, though it's

emotionally draining? Open a yoga studio, in spite of iffy income? Or, try to do both? (Which would be exhausting.)

Further, I'm afraid to leave escorting entirely. Unlike every above-ground job I've ever had, as an adult-companion I can confidently count on having money to buy food, pay dental and other medical bills, help with my sons' college costs — and still have enough left over to pay rent at the end of the month.

So, even though I now have a BA, an MPA, and an MSW, I continue to feel anxious and undecided about my future.

In sum, nothing is really ready for prime time except my escort website. And yet, I'm now 43 — it's past time to move on from escorting.

Drug Counseling in the South Bronx

While working for SWU 75, I meet Jason, a supervisor and therapist at a South Bronx mental health clinic. Since I've already mentioned that I'm fluent in Spanish, when I tell him the therapists at SWU 75 are being laid off, he suggests, "Why don't you send me your résumé?"

After sending it in, I soon get called in for an interview, and then I'm hired!

I'll be working in a program for mentally ill chemical abusers (MICA). The starting pay is $49,000/year, plus benefits — almost twice what I've ever made before in a regular job. It's within my area of training, and it'll be good experience.

I start in late summer 2002. For awhile, I enjoy the work. But eventually, I realize that I can't be of much help to clients who are schizophrenic. It's a tough slog.

In fact, the whole work environment is tough in another sense. During this era, there's gunfire even during the day in the South Bronx, because street gangs have "initiation shootings", ie, they shoot up places as a rite of passage.

There are streetwalkers strolling by our building to make drug money. Shockingly, the *vocational counselor* is a pimp on the side! He comes to our team meetings, counts his hundred dollar bills in front of us, and makes comments like, "My girls did really good today."

I feel like part of the craziness myself. Here *I* am, a social worker during the day in a dangerous low-income neighborhood, but on some nights I'm an escort going to a 5-star hotel to be wined and dined by a wealthy client. (Naturally, when I'm at work I don't talk to anyone about these dates.)

Between my own escort work and the vocational counselor having streetwalkers working for him, I think, *This is nuts!* But, once again, it's part of the inevitable duality of life.

Overall, the *whole team* is a little strange. John has been there about 20 years, and is avidly awaiting retirement. Larry is constantly yelling at clients; he too is waiting to retire. Marion is in her 50's, and seems very frustrated that she's still single. She rubs me the wrong way — all the time. Then there's Laquan, a substance-abuse counselor who at the same time is an active heroin addict. One time I see him in the office with blood running down his arm!

It's very confusing. Which world is more absurd — my night job or my day job? I think it raises a lot of questions about society, and how we as a people deal with the most vulnerable among us.

An Office Of My Own

I work at the MICA program for about 15 months. Toward the end of my time there, I start looking for office space in order to go out on my own.

I've been thinking that Astoria would be a good place to open a practice. It's the Queens neighborhood where I raised my sons, so it's familiar territory. And, as a mainly working class neighborhood, it's largely underserved by social services, compared with many other NYC neighborhoods. So, it becomes my goal to provide psychotherapy to the Astoria community.

In 2002, I speak with Raffaelle, who owns a local pizzeria. (As mentioned, in our darkest days Raffaelle often gave me and my sons a free pizza.) I say to him, "I'm looking for office space. Do you know of any that's available?"

He replies, "I know an optometrist who might sublet part of his space."

The optometrist's name is Ken. I visit him at his office suite. He tells me, "I have a psychotherapist tenant, Harvey, who rents a small office here. He comes in just once a week; maybe he'll let you sublet from him the other days."

When I ask Harvey, he replies, "That won't be a problem. But, Astoria isn't a good place for a psychotherapy practice. I own a very successful counseling center in Kew Gardens. Why don't you come work for me there?"

I say, "Alright, but I also want my own practice in Astoria."

Harvey responds, "That's fine — you do your thing. I don't want to come here anymore, because there's so little business in this neighborhood. You can sublet my office here — I don't really need it. But, come to Kew Gardens and work for me too."

So, I start working for Harvey for 4, sometimes 5, days a week in Kew Gardens, plus 1 day a week for myself in Astoria. Ken charges me $100 a month for the Astoria office, which is very low rent by New York standards.

Therapy Mills

Harvey is running "therapy mills" in both Kew Gardens and Rego Park. He has about 20 therapists working for him in Kew Gardens alone. The clients aren't screened, and the therapists aren't supervised by a more senior therapist.

His whole operation has a revolving door vibe that feels similar to Magda's, except that she had a lot more empathy for her clients than Harvey's office staff does. It's just a job for them. Unlike Magda's, they don't care about the clients' well-being, or that of the therapists. For example, at Harvey's no one advises the therapist if a new client is violent, or suicidal, or has recently been hospitalized.

So, I never know what I'll be dealing with when I meet a client for the 1st time. But I do learn how to run the business end of a practice. And, perhaps more importantly, how *not* to run the counseling end.

I work for Harvey for just a year — fall 2002 to fall 2003. Supposedly, he's been paying me half of what the insurance companies have paid him. But, I'm never shown what the insurer has actually remitted. Given the whole money-driven feel of his operation, I suspect that Harvey is underpaying me. I'd see 40, 50, 60 clients a week — as many as 12 clients a day, 5 days a week. Yet I earn only around $50,000 during that year. Harvey's gross per therapist is at least as much (probably more), and he has 20 therapists — just in Kew Gardens. In a sense, it's like pimping, but much more lucrative. Otherwise, not very different.

In October 2003, I give Harvey notice that I'm leaving, because I'm getting evermore calls in Astoria (even though Harvey was unable to generate much business there). I no longer have enough time to work in both Harvey's practice and my own. I decide to take the plunge. I've already quit the MICA program in the South Bronx, so now I'm flying solo as a counselor.

Sex Ok-Boyfriend not Ok

Fear of Dating

By late 2003, my life is finally going smoothly. I have my own growing practice as a counselor, and I'm back living in Astoria. I'm escorting very little these days — just a few longtime clients. I haven't romantically dated since 2000, but as noted, some of my escorting regulars have become platonic friends. It all feels okay to me. Why should I go on conventional dates, not knowing what kind of relationship I might wind up getting trapped in?

When I go on an escorting call, in most cases the client is a gentleman who treats me as a (very nice) social date would — but with no further strings attached. After the date, I just go home. No worries. And of course, I've made some money.

My biggest fear of social dating is that I'll meet another Marco. I have such a poor track record that I don't trust myself. I've often been attracted to men who are sexy and interesting (like father). Often they've turned out to be abusive and dangerous (like father). So, maybe this will seem a little twisted to readers, but I feel safer meeting paying clients than I do going on social dates — *much* safer.

And, to tell the truth, being an independent escort can be exciting. Further, it's doubly exciting to be a social worker during the day, come home and change from an office-professional outfit into something glamorous, and feel like I'm a totally different person when I join a client at a nice restaurant.

Priorities

As mentioned, my longer-term goal is to not be poor in America when I'm old (something mother always feared would happen to her). In my past social life, I've been un-healthily promiscuous with men I shouldn't have been with at all. And, I've done other things that were impulsive and unwise. When I woke up from my on-again/off-again heroin stupor, I had to face the reality that my sons and I were so poor because I'd squandered my inheritance from father. Once we had nothing, and father and mother were both gone forever, it was a really sobering experience for me.

I now ask myself, *Should I continue dating socially — and end up old with nothing? Or, do I want to set some goals and work towards them?*

So romantic sex isn't that important during this period in my life. In my website business, sex is only a means to an end. Yes, there are times when a web-client is also a good lover. But it's a 1- or 2-hour frolic, nothing more than that.

I don't consume a drop of alcohol with a client in all those years. Tara and Debbie sometimes get sidetracked on a date — drinking wine and maybe spending a few hours with a really hot guy. They sort of drift away, because they've had too much to drink. I say to myself, *The heck with that! I'm not drinking, and I'm not getting high. We have a deal: You pay me for a fixed amount of time — then I'm gone.*

I have to be practical. Debbie and Tara, like many other webscorts, don't have children. Whereas, I have family obligations. People who have only themselves to worry about can come and go as they please. But, even though my sons aren't little anymore, they still need my help at times.

Jamie Lee Curtis said something like: There's an incredible amount of self-knowledge that comes with getting older. Despite my messing-up for the first 25 years of my life, I've been able to catch up to the point where most people have no idea what I've actually gone through.

It's another example of how we judge each other. People may see me as a therapist who has it all together. Maybe they think I've been privileged all of my life, so I won't be able to understand their situation. In fact I've been through most of what my clients have been through, and then some.

Realities

I think there's something in all of us that yearns for a romantic relationship with a special someone who meets our every need. We want a best friend, great communicator, kindred spirit, amazing sex partner, and yet still have the freedom to be oneself and come and go as we please. But, it's rare for 2 people to find all of that with only each other — right up to the end.

Dr. Keith Ablow is a forensic psychiatrist and author. I like much of what he has to say. For example, he's written that though magnetic objects attract each other at first, if they stay attached to one another for too long, their attraction wanes. It's similar with the chemistry in relationships. After a couple has been together for 5 to 10 years, a lot of the fizz has fizzled out.

Though they may still deeply love each other, perhaps one partner wants to experiment by trying something new. Yet often, for one reason or another, it's not possible to try something new with their life-partner.

So, some people choose a person outside of their committed relationship to explore with. Someone they feel safe with. Often it's in a paid relationship that a man finds a woman, or a man, with whom he feels safe to explore his secret passions. Then he goes home and loves his wife and children, just as before.

I have a lot more respect for that man than for one who has a romantic affair with a co-worker, making himself the apex of a love-triangle. To me, that's a lot more damaging than visiting an escort in a different city every few months when he travels there on business. If my husband or boyfriend did something like that, it would bother me much less than if he were having an affair with a neighbor or a friend — or worse a relative, like Fabio did with my cousin Astrid. That is much more painful, because he's bringing his affair into my backyard. (More about this to come.)

Departure

As noted, I have to push myself a little to completely give up escorting. Part of me enjoys the freedom of being an indie, needing only a few appointments weekly to provide a financial cushion for my family and me. It's been a comforting safety net. But I ask myself, *What will I do when I'm no longer young enough for this? I went to school for so many years. If I don't stay focused on a career as a counselor, what am I going to do when I hit 45? Or 50? Eventually, I'm not going to be that physically desirable anymore. As a therapist, it won't matter if I'm 60, 70, or even 80 — as long as I still have my mental faculties.*

𝔐𝔶 𝔏𝔞𝔰𝔱 𝔥𝔲𝔰𝔟𝔞𝔫𝔡!

To this day, I keep in touch with friends and family living in South Tyrol. If one of them has a friend who is coming to NYC, she might send her friend my way.

For example, in the latter half of 2003 I get a phone call from my South Tyrolean friend Tristan. She tells me a friend of hers, Dagmar, is going to be in NYC for a few months, and asks if Dagmar can stay with me. I've got an empty bedroom, because my sons are both out of the house by then, so I agree.

Dagmar arrives on a cold night in late fall, and stays several months (paying a bit for rent). I want to show her New York, and since she is 22 or 23, I take her clubbing a few times.

China Club

Sometime in January 2004, Dagmar and I go dancing at the China Club, a trendy place in downtown Manhattan. Early on, I agree to dance with a guy who turns out to be very pushy and annoying. I'm not attracted to him at all, and I want to get away from him. But he won't stop following me around.

Suddenly, I see a really confident-looking man with a big smile on his face who's striding straight toward me. He isn't tall — about 5′ 8″ — yet with complete self-assurance he asks me if I'd dance with him.

I'm happy he's come to my rescue, because I want to get away from this other guy. We start dancing. I think he's kind of cute. I've never met a man built like him — his whole body seems like solid muscle.

But, I don't like the way he's holding me. His arms feel like Iron Man's, and he's way too forceful, almost hurting me. My sense is that he's a klutz who doesn't know how a man should dance with a woman. I say to him, "You're holding my neck too tight — you're hurting me." He just laughs and keeps doing the same thing. So I say, "Let's sit down."

A Really Nice Guy

His name is Ramón, and he's from Peru. I think, *Uh-oh, this isn't a good omen. Marco is from Peru.* Then he tells me he's studying taekwondo, also like Marco. I think, *This isn't reassuring either!*

But Ramón is very friendly, endearingly so. He jokes a lot while we talk. He's 12 years younger than I am (by this time, I'm 45). He's an immigrant (like me), and he works in construction. Since he also lives in Queens, at the end of the night I say to him, "If you want a ride home, Dagmar and I will take you."

He accepts my offer, and while I'm driving him home, I get the feeling he's a really nice guy — the opposite of Marco. There's something about Ramón that is sweet and childlike. I feel that, in spite of his awkwardness as a dancer, maybe he'd be a good person to go out with.

Though I don't see Ramón again right away, we talk on the phone a few times. Eventually, I accept his invitation to meet for dinner. (Fortunately, for reasons that will be seen, it's not an expensive restaurant.)

Ramón turns out to be different from every other man I've known, in the sense that if I mention that I need help with something, he immediately offers his assistance. And he doesn't just *offer* help, he actually *helps.* This is a big difference from the rest. Until Ramón, I've never had a man in my life whom I could ask, "Would you take out the garbage?" — and he'd actually do it!

Since father died, I haven't had someone who's there for me, who'll reliably follow up on promises. I haven't had much help at all, until Ramón comes into my life. Now, whatever I need, I can always count on him.

I also like that he's super energetic, and incredibly driven. And yet, he's humble (or so he seems in the beginning).

Plus, Ramón has a really strong work ethic — just the opposite of Marco (a parasite who wanted everything for free, and felt *entitled* to it). When we meet back in January, Ramón is riding his bicycle in the cold to go to work each day. Being undocumented at the time, he's a $50 per day worker at construction sites, or in garment industry sweatshops.

He soon becomes like a personal trainer for me. We run together in the park, which is something I really enjoy. And, because of his encouragement, he helps me get emotionally, as well as physically, stronger.

As noted, Ramón himself is very fit and strong. He has a military background, having been in the Peruvian Army's special forces. And, he has completed a US Navy SEAL training course (which he's very proud of). Overall, Ramón isn't an average guy. And, he's nice to boot — never yelling, never abusive. He seems to be a genuinely good person.

I Sort of Fall in Love With Ramón

Though we keep growing closer, my feelings for Ramón are not quite like those a woman has for a lover. And yet, in a sense I do love him. I think it's because we're alike in so many ways. We enjoy doing things together socially, plus we get a lot accomplished when working as a team. Often we complement each other. When I have an idea, he supports me. And if he gets an idea, I support him.

Although I feel a strong emotional attachment, I'm not attracted to him in a sexual way. He's actually kind of annoying when it comes to physical intimacy. As when he dances, the way he holds me at other times is clumsy — even painful. He definitely lacks the ability to sense when a woman needs a gentle touch. He'd hug me so hard that it'd feel almost as if he's choking me.

But, it's clear that Ramón doesn't mean to hurt me. He's just a country boy who lacks polish. And yet, he's very intelligent (again, unlike Marco). He's read some Plato and Aristotle. He also practices yoga. Plus, to my surprise, he knows a lot about European history.

Still, although smart and pretty well educated, he lacks sophistication. In a way, his naiveté is another thing that makes him likable. (Yet, in combination with his physical aggressiveness, it eventually leads to his downfall.)

But again, Ramón's most outstanding quality is his unfailing willingness to help out. No matter what I need or want, he tries his best to be there for me — from building a closet, to painting walls, to making sure my car is running.

For example, one time my car had a flat tire at 11 o'clock at night. Though at that point he still had only a bicycle, he pedaled his way to where I was located to put on a spare tire for me. Ramón is almost like the brother that I've never had. He gives me a sense that he's going to be a life-partner who will be there for me, no matter what, for just about anything — even polishing my shoes!

As will be discussed in more detail below, Ramón encourages me to hire more therapists in order to grow my practice as a psychotherapist. Beyond just words of encouragement, he's a great help in renovating a bigger and much better space for me.

Within a year after meeting him, we open 2 businesses: Astoria Wellness Center, a counseling facility; and Astoria Hot Yoga, a yoga studio. At the start, Ramón manages the yoga business, and I run the counseling practice.

Without Ramón, I could never have opened Astoria Hot Yoga. Though projects sometimes aren't as easy as he made them sound, he always does make them happen. Overall, he makes me confident I can accomplish much more in life.

We often go out to eat together. We have a favorite Mexican restaurant, and we also go to steakhouses and restaurants featuring Peruvian, Greek, or American cuisine.

Ramón is good company and he's available on short notice. I don't have other friends whom I can call in the afternoon and say, "Let's go to dinner" — and they'll be able to join me. They typically say something like, "I really can't tonight. We'll have to plan it."

Everything in New York has to be *planned.* It's so annoying. No one can be spontaneous. A get-together must be penciled-in weeks in advance. Then, just before the scheduled date arrives, people often cancel and the event has to be rescheduled — about 2 months later!

Like me, Ramón could act on the spur of the moment. He'd call and ask, "Are you hungry? Let's go out to dinner."

And I'd answer, "Sure, let's go."

Since we're both spontaneous (and driven to succeed), we understand each other (on that score).

This Is Why We Can't Go To Nice Places

But, the downside of Ramón's spontaneity is his impulsiveness. And, the problem with his lack of sophistication is his occasionally creating a public scene.

For example, after we've known each other about a year, I take him to an expensive restaurant in Astoria to celebrate his birthday.

Ramón (who loves meat) orders lamb chops. The server brings 2 small lamb chops, a dab of mashed potatoes, and a smallish portion of vegetables. Ramón calls back the server to complain that he hasn't gotten enough food. I feel very embarrassed, and say to him, "I will *never* take you to a nice restaurant again."

And yet, I don't think Ramón had bad intentions. He's been raised in poverty, so he feels an expensive restaurant ought to serve bigger portions than an inexpensive restaurant. He doesn't take into account that if the quality of the food is much better, a smaller portion will still cost more.

On the other hand, his intentions aren't always so innocent. I get us tickets to see Madonna in concert. Our seats are high up in the mezzanine. But before the concert begins, Ramón wants us to switch seats. He insists, "Come on, come on, let's go down to the orchestra section. There'll be seats that aren't taken."

I object, "I can't do that. I'm an adult — not a teenager. I won't switch seats just to see Madonna close up, when I can see her on the video screen. So what if I'm not sitting right in front of her? I don't need to be that close."

But, *no* — he has to drag *me* with him. So now we're stealing 2 seats. When the people who've paid for the seats arrive, naturally they want them. Ramón makes a big scene, aggressively insisting, "No, these are *our* seats!"

I plead with him, "Ramón, they're going to get Security. Let's go back to our real seats." He refuses. I get angry, "Why are you doing this? Do you want Security to kick us out? Move your butt off these seats. They aren't ours. We didn't pay for them — let's go back to where we should be sitting."

So, even fun things can be dicey with Ramón, because he'd break the rules and do whatever he wants. Meanwhile, I'm thinking, *How can he feel this is okay?!*

Ramón makes me anxious in a lot of situations. There are times when he just *wants* to create a scene — especially in restaurants. He has grown up jumping off horses barefoot and living like a wild-child. Now that he's in New York, on some level he wants to wear big boots. But NYC boots are too big for his feet — he can't really fill them.

Further, Ramón doesn't know how to drink responsibly in social settings. Because liquor is free at parties, he drinks until he's in a blackout, or starts puking, or is so wasted that he falls asleep sitting in a chair. I'd say to him, "Just because it's free, that doesn't mean you have to drink to the point of alcohol poisoning. Stop after a few drinks. You aren't even enjoying this anymore — you pass out and fall off the chair, or vomit. How much fun is that?

In many ways, Ramón is a tough warrior. But, sometimes he has a spoiled sense of entitlement. Because he so often creates some sort of uproar in public, I start to avoid going out with him. Eventually, I stop going to places with him entirely. When he calls and asks, "Do you want dinner?", I answer, "No, that's okay, I'm tired."

And yet I can't stay mad at him, because he has such a childlike way about him. He'd smile at me and say, "I know, I'm sorry, I made a mistake — but do you still love me?"

Shared Abandonment Issues

In a certain way, our childhoods were similar. Even though my father was wealthy, and his family was poor, we both came from broken homes, and were, in effect, abandoned by the parent of the same sex.

Ramón was born out-of-wedlock. But his father then married another woman — not Ramón's mother. (Oddly, he named his son from this marriage "Ramón" also.) So, Ramón has always felt discarded by his father, just as I've always felt discarded by my mother.

One time his (usually absent) father promised him a bicycle, and then brought him a broken one. Ramón says that's the only present he ever got from his father.

Ramón was instead raised by lots of women. His mother had 4 or 5 sisters, and his grandmother was in the picture too. At any given time, there were always 1 or 2 women taking care of him. When he visited an aunt, she'd cook for him. If she got mad at him, he'd leave and go visit another aunt. If he got into trouble there, he'd go see his grandmother. So, he always had as a safety net a female relative who'd meet his needs.

It's at this emotional level that our upbringings chiefly differed. I grew up without anyone who really took care of my needs as a child. Someone with whom I felt wanted, safe, and at ease.

My Aunt Marthe (father's brother's wife) did help me a bit. Yet, she'd also make it clear that I was a 5th wheel on the wagon. For example, she'd say things like, "You can eat here, but you can't have any meat. The meat is for my husband and my children." (What I didn't appreciate as a child is that she'd endured strict meat rationing throughout 2 world wars.)

Fortunately, I don't even *like* meat. I'd reply to her, "It's okay, I'll just eat rice and gravy."

So, unlike me, Ramón got lots of familial love from women. But, like me, there were alcoholic adults present in his youth. Further, he was sexually abused by an older male cousin. (Ramón reveals this later on in our relationship.)

Growing Up Andean

Still, Ramón often played alone, in his youth (like me). His grandmother had a horse she'd let him ride, and Ramón would jump on it, gallop up a hill, and throw himself off the horse. Then, he'd jump back on the horse and do it again. He'd do this for hours on end, for the sheer fun of it.

Something Ramón enjoyed doing with a group of friends was jumping into a nearby river, floating downstream (to the electric generator it fed), and then swimming back upstream. It was like the rivers people float along in a Disney River Park, except the river Ramón and his friends played in carried them downstream very rapidly. It was incredible physical exercise, and they'd do it all day long.

So Ramón too grew up surrounded by nature, getting lots of exercise, and running about in bare feet. But, unlike me, he was barefoot because he was too poor to have shoes.

Another difference is that he grew up knowing how to kill a chicken, clean it, and then eat it the same night. He also learned how to take care of other farm animals.

Yet, I still identify a good deal with Ramón's upbringing. We both grew up in a small town surrounded by mountains, loving the outdoors, running around in nature, feeling free (and without much discipline). And, we both lacked a loving nuclear family.

One time I ask Ramón which relative from his childhood I represent in his life. He answers that I remind him of his grandmother, since she's the one who loved him the most.

Ghost Buster

At some point in our relationship, the usually cheerful Ramón confides in me that he fears things are never going to improve for him in America. He's willing to work very hard, but he feels like a ghost, because he doesn't have valid papers. He came here legally on a tourist visa, but has long since overstayed (like I did).

Ramón's goal all along has been to join the American military, because he greatly admires the US armed forces. And, as noted, he received Navy SEAL training while he was a Ranger in the Peruvian military. But, he needs to be a permanent US resident in order to enlist. So, I say to him, "I have an idea. I'm willing to marry you and help you apply for your papers." And so, we get married in June 2004 — just 5 months after we met.

As with my marriage to Marco, I don't tell anyone, not even my sons. They wouldn't have understood. Unless you're an adult immigrant, you don't realize how hard it is to make a living without papers.

My sons were young children when they came to America, so they've grown up here. They haven't gone through the struggle I went through as an immigrant. I protected them by making sure they both became US citizens. I wanted to be certain they'd never be deported back to a country they had no memory of.

Ramón and I hire an immigration lawyer, because this time I don't want to go through what I went through with Marco's application. Because we made so many mistakes, a lot of time was wasted. (As mentioned, in the end I withdrew my sponsorship of Marco, because of his stalking.)

Since leaving my job as a social worker at Manhattan Family in 2000, I've stayed in contact with some of the people I worked with there. One of them is Dave, a very good psychiatrist who supervised me. His wife, Adele, is an excellent therapist also. A few of us who worked together go out for dinner every 2 or 3 months. Over dinner one evening, Adele suggests, "If you need an immigration lawyer, call Mitch. He's one of the best in the city."

In August 2004, Ramón and I visit Mitch's fancy office in a building on Madison Avenue. We apply for Ramón's papers during our 1st appointment.

After that, everything goes smoothly. Two months later, we already have our 1st interview with INS. Many people wait 2 or 3 years for their interview. Yet, it all happens quickly for Ramón. It's as if the stars are aligned so that everything will come to Ramón easily (too easily, as things turn out).

The interview with INS goes very well. I've studied his family, he's studied my family, we have pictures, bank accounts — anything INS might want to see.

They don't doubt us at all, though often if the woman is older, or if an immigrant person of color marries a white partner, INS suspects they've married just for the green card. In our case, they have reason for suspicion on both counts. I'm Austro-German and pale, whereas Ramón is Peruvian and swarthy. Second, I'm 12 years older than he is. And yet, as with my 2 previous husbands, it isn't a sham marriage. We're really trying to make a go of it.

In February 2005, 6 months after applying, Ramón gets his green card. I've never heard of such speed!

By now I care about Ramón a lot. I'm not crazy about him physically. As mentioned, he's kind of pushy and klutzy. But he's otherwise so nice, and he helps me in so many ways, that I've come to feel very close to him emotionally.

Yoga Teacher

Ramón moves in with me as soon as we marry. Since he hasn't gotten his papers yet, I suggest, "Instead of working for $50 a day in construction, why not become a yoga teacher? If you teach 2 or 3 classes in a day, at $50 a class, you'll make $100 or $150 — and no one will ask to see your papers. Plus, it's a better way of making a living than killing yourself with a sledgehammer, and breathing in dust and cement all day long.

Ramón agrees, so I pay the fees for him to take a hot-yoga training course in Florida. Although he hardly speaks English at the time, Ramón is game. He uses a dictionary to study English daily. Plus, he watches movies and television, and listens to pop song lyrics — anything that will improve his English-language skills.

On Craigslist, we find a Florida man who has a little trailer for rent. It looks ideal in the photo, so Ramón flies to Florida and, after meeting the man, rents it. For the next 6 weeks, Ramón rollerblades every day to the hotel where the yoga training takes place — about 5 or 6 miles each way.

Because he has so much energy and drive, no obstacle is too great for Ramón. If he has to climb up and down a mountain every day to achieve his goal, he will do it. This is what impresses me most about him. He can go far, and we can go far together, because we're both very driven. When we set goals as a team, we make them happen.

He gets back from Florida in December 2004, and as noted, 2 months later he gets his green card. So now, it's perfectly legal for him to be teaching yoga here in the US.

I hook him up with a few of my contacts. Soon he has a regular job teaching yoga. It turns out that he's very good at it. Ramón has a solid physique, plus prior teaching experience as a diving instructor in the Peruvian Army. Even though his English still isn't that great, students seek out his yoga classes, because they really like him.

The Little Farm in the Valley

Now that he has his green card, Ramón can leave the US and return again without a problem. We decide to go to Peru to visit his family (a sort of delayed honeymoon). In April 2005, we fly to Lima, Peru's capital. (Ramón leaves a few days before I do — to meet some "friends" — the significance of which I don't realize until later.)

It turns out to be quite an adventure! From Lima, we take a bus up into the mountains. The Pacific Ocean is on one side, and desert-like mountains of sand are on the other. I've never seen a landscape like this. Once we're near the top of the mountain, there's an oasis, rich with trees and other greenery. This is where he grew up.

Ramón's family are all amazing! They have a small farm in a little valley surrounded by the barren mountains. They grow mangoes, grapes, avocados, and other fruits. It's all so beautiful — really nice.

I now can see how Ramón grew up. The house doesn't have man-made flooring — there's hard-packed dirt beneath our feet. Two or 3 people sleep in a bed, 1 with their head pointing one way; the other 1 or 2 with their head in the opposite direction (an arrangement still common in many places).

Ramón's family is quite close, and they're very nice to me too. They each give me a present. And, they kill a chicken and lay out a huge feast on an enormous wooden table in our honor. Everyone comes. Every cousin. Every child. Every aunt and uncle, including the mentally ill uncle and the alcoholic aunt. I get the sense that I'm part of a family now, which is a feeling I've never had before. The children love me, and they call me either "aunt" or "cousin". It's a really warm and wonderful experience.

Climbing to Machu Picchu

Machu Picchu is a fabulous estate built by an Incan king in the mid-1400's atop Guiana Picchu, a mountain in the Andes. It's some 1½ miles above sea level, about half again as high in the sky as Denver, Colorado. Ramón, his mother, and I fly there. It's a really fascinating trip — probably one of the best trips of my life. It takes about an hour to make the steep climb up Guiana Picchu to get to Machu Picchu. (The pathway isn't safe, so I really have to be careful. Otherwise it might be my last climb.)

Though I'm getting exhausted climbing up the mountain (in spite of my daily exercise routine), Ramón is like a goat *running* up the mountain! It amazes me that he's so strong and has so much energy. (He kind of teases me along the way, because it's taking me so much longer than it's taking him.)

The Look Of Mormon

While we're making the climb, Ramón suddenly notices 2 young men who "seem" American. We soon learn they're Mormons who've come from the US to evangelize for their faith (in accordance with their religion's requirements). Ramón starts excitedly talking to them in his broken English, asking if he can take their picture with his phone. Watching this, I wonder *What's up with him?*

Why "YMCA"?

Even before we go to Peru, I start to wonder if Ramón is bisexual. He loves all the disco music from the 70's and 80's — Donna Summer, Backstreet Boys, Village People. And, not just every so often. He'd listen to "YMCA" and "In the Navy" over and over and over. I'm like, *Are you serious?*

Also, the way he often dresses is not the way most straight guys typically dress. He likes wearing pink shirts. Or, baby blue. Sometimes he'd ask to wear one of *my* shirts!

If I'd say something like, "That shirt's kind of feminine," he'd reply, "No, I just like it."

Again, it's not just occasionally — it's much of the time. Different things start to emerge that have me saying to myself, *This is odd.*

At one point, he wants me to go with him to the Church of Scientology in Manhattan, because Tom Cruise is going to be there. Ramón gets dressed up in his best Sunday outfit. Since I don't care about Tom Cruise *or* the Church of Scientology, I decline. Ramón goes by himself — hoping to meet Tom Cruise.

He'd sit at the computer and watch YouTube videos of Chayanne, a Latin American pop star. Chayanne is a really gorgeous man, and Ramón would watch one of Chayanne's videos, "Torero" (bullfighter), countless times — to the point that I become nauseous. I'd sometimes ask, "Can we listen to something else?!"

Ramón would reply, "When I was in Peru, I watched Chayanne all the time. I learned to dance the way he does, because I like it so much." (Unfortunately for my stepped-on toes, Ramón doesn't have Chayanne's *talent* for dancing.)

He also loves Madonna, so we wind up going to see her in concert (as described earlier).

Now that we're in Peru, I meet Ramón's grandmother, who is about 85. She seems to have a thousand wrinkles on her face, like a photo in *National Geographic*. But, her mind is sharp. She says to me, "I'm so happy Ramón finally got married, because I was sure he's gay."

His relatives are even talking about us having babies. At this point I'm already 46. I'm not having more babies! But they are happily anticipating our having a baby soon anyway.

When we go to a restaurant in Lima, Ramón introduces me to his friend Armand, a lawyer in the Peruvian military. Armand is around my age — in his mid-40's. Ramón is 34 at this point. He tells me Armand was his sugar daddy when he was 18, and he dated him for a time. Armand even bought Ramón a Mustang sports car(!) — among other expensive gifts.

So Ramon is now admitting he once had an ongoing intimate relationship with another man. I ask him, "Are you still attracted to men?"

Ramón guardedly replies, "What if I *am* gay?"

I respond, "Well if you're gay, that's okay with me. Don't try to force yourself to be something you're not. I just want to know what's up?"

But, Ramón says he will never identify as gay. He wishes he were different. He can't accept his attraction to men, and he's really fighting it. He wants to have a family in the worst way. (So he's dating other women, as I later learn.)

While on our visit, I learn that Ramón is still popular in the Peruvian Army. A lot of military people there know and like him. I get the sense from Ramón that he worked his way up the ranks in part by spending some of his time on the military version of the "casting couch".

For now, I let the matter rest. His plan all along has been to join the US Army. Once he leaves for a career in the military, his sex life will no longer be my concern.

Something Else We Have In Common

As mentioned, Ramón was sexually abused as a child, by an older male cousin. So, as an adult, Ramón doesn't emotionally connect to people through sex. I don't think his heart is hooked up to his genitals.

Sex isn't what draws us together. We do have intimate relations, but our sex isn't anything special. In fact, I've had much better sex with some of my clients as an escort.

And yet, though I realize that Ramón isn't emotionally present during sex, it doesn't really bother me. Because, at the end of the day, I've never had a romantic relationship where it all comes together: We can be ourselves, feel supported and loved, plus have great chemistry in and out of bed. (Perhaps not many couples have the whole package.)

With Ramón, it's much more important to me than sex that he's there for me when I need him. Someone whom, as noted, I can call at 11 o'clock at night and say, "I have a flat tire", and he'll come help me, no matter what it takes.

Hearing Loss

When we get back to America, it's still spring 2005. Ramón begins to study in earnest for the US Army's written exam. His English isn't yet very good. But, he diligently reads for hours on end, and takes many practice tests.

Ramón does pass the written test. But, because of field exercises with artillery and dynamite during his dozen years in the Peruvian Army, he's had some hearing loss. It doesn't impair him in civilian life. But, the US Army rejects him because of it. He feels crushed by this — really, really upset. He has so wanted to be part of that big machine.

His whole life plan has evaporated. He was hoping to fight in Iraq. He's the kind of man who would've enjoyed combat duty. In civilian life, he feels like a fish out of water. He loves the military: the challenges, adventures, brotherhood, and all the rest. (Also, I think the fact that there are many handsome men in the military is part of its appeal for him.)

Seeking Sunlight; Getting Gaslight

As noted, until he failed the Army's hearing test, I assumed that Ramón would eventually be more or less out of my life. Now that we will be together longer than either of us had planned, I want more clarity in our relationship than I felt was necessary back when we were in Peru.

One day when we're in the kitchen, I confront him, "I need to know if you've been hiding something from me, because I'm starting to feel a little crazy. I've noticed so many hints, like your taste in clothing and music, and the celebrities you seem to worship. And, I know enough about sex to know you're not emotionally present when we have sex. So, I've been wondering if you're gay?"

Ramón doesn't answer directly. Instead, he replies with a question, like he did when we were in Peru: "What if I *am?*"

I respond, "Well, if you are, a lot of stuff makes more sense, and I won't feel like I'm crazy. I'll respect you if you're honest with me. If you're gay, you're gay. We can still have a close relationship, but it'll have to be platonic." (I doubt that he's practicing safe sex with other partners.)

He then asks me, "If I said I'm gay, would you judge me? Would you look at me differently?"

I answer, "No, I won't judge you. In fact, I'll support you. But, I don't want to be lied to. I've been feeling really nuts about this. I've had this sense that there's something going on, but you won't tell me what, and it's been keeping me off-balance."

At this point, I feel the cat is finally out of the bag.

But he continues to insist, "I'll never be openly gay. I'd rather die. It'd be so embarrassing. It'd be the worst thing."

Ramón's been raised in a religiously conservative country, where gays are very stigmatized. Plus, these religious beliefs make him fear that he's going to hell. I think this is why he's doing everything he can to convince the world, and himself, that he's a heterosexual playboy.

For awhile, Ramón and I continue to be very close emotionally, because I believe he's being honest with me. I assume the many phone calls he gets are only from *men* he's dating. But when I find out he's dating women too, I'm very upset. Do these women know Ramón is having sex with several men, and if so, whether he's having *safe* sex with them?

Although I'm beginning to back away emotionally, I say to him, "We can still be friends and partners. We work well together, so we can open a yoga studio if you're willing."

Ramón is all for it. He'd love to have a yoga studio with me.

(Too) Hot Yoga

It's now early summer 2005. My older son Lukas's best friend since their elementary school days died in a car accident a couple of months earlier. He'd just left a bar — after 2 AM. It's a devastating loss for Lukas, who was sharing an apartment with his friend at the time.

Partly for this reason, I feel it would be a good idea to open a yoga studio in Astoria. The neighborhood needs an outlet besides bars. Maybe a yoga studio would get young people involved in something healthier than drinking. And, maybe yoga would help them become more aware in general.

Working as a team, Ramón and I find a raw space that's available for very little rent — because it's in terrible shape. The rooms are filthy, and there's debris everywhere.

Ramón looks it over and asks, "You like it?"

I answer, "Well, I do have a vision for it. The amount of floor space would make a great yoga studio, and it has a basement, so we'd have storage space. Plus, it has a backyard. But, it needs a lot of work just to clean up, and we'd have to build a shower."

Ramón responds, "It's no problem. I'll build all of this for you. I'll build you a shower. I'll put a new floor in the basement. I'll build you a *castle* — anything you want, I'll build it for you."

I look at him and ask, "Really? We can do this?"

He replies, "You want a yoga studio? Then we'll do it!"

As discussed earlier, Ramón isn't someone who just talks the talk. As soon as I rent the space, he proceeds to renovate the floors and the walls. He builds a bathroom with a shower. He puts benches and huge flowerpots in the back. He hangs the mirrors and the light fixtures. He builds windows. He does it all — an incredible amount of work.

Ramón is also very creative in going about it. He saves us a lot of money by doing the work himself, and by being extra thrifty. For example, he uses scrap wood from building one item to build others. On a South American budget, everything gets used — no waste. I admire that.

Yet, though we're on a very tight budget, Ramón makes every obstacle seem easy to overcome. For example:

Ramón: "We need sheet rock."

Me: "How're we going to transport sheet rock?"

Ramón: "We'll carry it on top of your Jeep."

So, we drive to Home Depot and buy ten 4′ x 8′ sheets. Ramón lifts the sheets up on top of the Jeep and ties them down. Then we drive to the studio, each of us with one arm out the window, holding onto the stack of sheet rock to keep the wind from causing the sheets to flop about. Along the way, we play music really loud, and Ramón is even louder singing over it. He has a way of making work fun!

Ramón labors on. He demolishes walls, then sweeps up the debris into Hefty bags. We can't afford our own dumpster. So every night Ramón drives around in the little Hyundai station wagon he owns by now, and I follow in my Jeep. We look for industrial-size containers, and dump into them the debris generated that day. Of course it's illegal — and kind of adolescent — but we don't have a practical alternative.

The back of Ramón's car is a mess, with his work boots, construction clothes, and dirty socks. But, he also has a change of clothes for going to clubs, including clean socks and multiple pairs of underwear. It's like a clothing closet in the trunk of his car. He'd stuff garbage bags in the back and then drive away to go dancing.

I'd be like, "Where on earth are you going?"

And he'd be like, "I'm going to find a container to dump the garbage. Then I'll change and go dancing. Don't worry — I have everything I need in the car."

"Seriously?! You just worked 12 hours, it's 1 o'clock in the morning, and you're going clubbing with bags of garbage in the car? *I'm* going to sleep!"

Like Ramón, I don't need to stand in front of the bathroom mirror for an hour to get ready. I can transform myself pronto. I know exactly what I need to put on. Even if I have only 5 minutes to get ready, I know where everything I'm going to wear is. So I can dress in a jiffy. I can look like a businessperson, a social escort for a high-income client, or a yoga teacher. It's almost like being a chameleon. I also eat very fast — I do everything fast! Yet, Ramón is a more extreme version of me as a quick-change artist. He'd change from one outfit to another within seconds.

As discussed, we are so similar in many ways that we really do have a close bond. Because Ramón has been so important in my life, I'd have gone through fire for him. But, little by little, I learn that he's badly damaged emotionally, and has some very troubling issues.

The Closing

Astoria Hot Yoga opens in the late summer or early fall of 2005. Since I don't need as much space now that Johan and Lukas have left home, to save time and money I move into a small 1-bedroom apartment Ramón has built atop the studio.

Unfortunately, the studio doesn't do very well. And, running it makes exhausting demands on my time, as well as my finances. These factors, in combination with Ramón's *too hot* behavior (more about this below), force me to close the studio in early 2007.

I feel sad, because I've put a lot of time and energy, as well as money, into the whole project. As noted, I was hoping the studio would help the overall community, and particularly Astoria's young people. Unfortunately, it doesn't accomplish either goal.

To avoid just shuttering the studio, I try to sell it. Adding to my disappointment, no one is interested in buying.

I then put an ad on Craigslist offering to give it away to any responsible party. A woman from an international yoga association contacts me, and says an affiliated group in nearby Jackson Heights would like to check out the studio.

Soon, a troupe of about 20 people come by — a sort of United Nations of Hare Krishna types. They love the space. Later, one of their leaders tells me they're interested in taking it over.

I feel good about this group. They're all very nice, so I give the studio to them. I'm glad Astoria still has a yoga studio, and that it's being run by a spiritually enlightened group of creative young people.

I continue to teach a class there. I don't charge for it, because I'm still interested in providing yoga to the community. I'm convinced that yoga has been very therapeutic for me, and I want to share this with my neighbors.

Sadly, the studio remains open only until late 2008 or early 2009. The woman who has been running it falls in love with an Australian man. They eventually marry and move there.

For awhile, a Buddhist monk provides meditation classes in the studio. But, that doesn't fly in Astoria. If yoga exercises aren't prospering, then sitting still and chanting isn't going to do well. Someone has to be at a certain spiritual level to be open to meditation and chanting. Usually people achieve that by working on their body before they are ready to meditate. And so, the studio closes its door for good.

It's around this time that I start to be less invested in changing Astoria. I'm not sure why I had that need in the 1st place. It may go back to my childhood in Bolzitano. As a small town, it had almost no social services. In Astoria, once again I'm in what may as well be a small town, even though it's technically part of NYC. There's another way it's similar to Bolzitano: lots of alcohol and drug abuse. I get a familiar feeling as I walk along Astoria Boulevard (a pretty depressing feeling).

On the other hand, Astoria does have a favorable side. I've been able to buy a house here with a nice backyard. We have privacy, and no one bothers us. It's almost like living in the country in the positive sense.

Why I Come to Love Ramón

Since we're so compatible, Ramón is almost my alter ego. I accomplish things with him that I've never accomplished with anyone else. He's like my perfect match in so many ways that eventually I do come to love him romantically.

I've already mentioned our midnight ride to get sheet rock from Home Depot. Another time, again at midnight, I tell Ramón I feel like replacing the kitchen floor. Right away he says, "Let's go!" — and off we go to the same 24-hour Home Depot. We pick out new tiles, pay for them, carry boxes and boxes of tiles out to the car, and get back home at 1 in the morning. Going the extra mile, night or day, is typical when I'm teamed-up with Ramón.

In 2008, he completely renovates the house I buy (with his help). It's absolutely unbelievable. No one else could accomplish what he does on a minimum budget. With Ramón, whether building the yoga studio or renovating my house, *everything* is doable. An American contractor would've said, *You want a shower? You need a permit.* In other words, lots of delays and extra expenses that would've made the project impossible for me to afford.

Transitioning

Ramón isn't just an indispensable partner in my construction projects. As mentioned above, he's good for me in other ways. I've never met anyone in my life who emotionally supported me the way he does. Who kept reassuring me that I'd achieve great things.

When I meet him in 2004, I've recently opened my private practice as a psychotherapist. Since I'm just starting out, I feel financially insecure. So, as noted, I'm still doing a little escorting on the side. Largely because of Ramón's constant reassurance, I gain the confidence to leave escorting completely.

He helps my personal growth in other ways. For example, he gets me to upgrade my daily workouts. Although I've never done push-ups in my life, with his encouragement I start doing them. And sit-ups too. He makes me feel like I can climb any mountain.

All of this is so important in my life. No one else ever encouraged me. No one else ever said, *You have the ability to accomplish your goals.*

Father always stood by me whenever I needed help. But, throughout my childhood, he'd undermine my confidence. When I cooked something, he might look into the pot and say, "Who can eat this crap?" If I knitted a sweater, he might say, "The farmer's daughter up on the mountain, *that girl* can knit — look at the beautiful sweater *she* made!"

It was never, "Marlena, you've done a good job." Never, ever.

What talents or strengths I might have, or what I'd like to do in life, weren't ever discussed. My only purpose in life, while growing up, was to be a caretaker for a father who had been psychologically damaged both by the war and by being abandoned by mother. I was his emotional crutch. He was my ball and chain. I wasn't allowed to be an individual, to have needs of my own.

As noted, Ramón is the 1st (and only) person in my life who gives me the sense that I will overcome every obstacle. He makes everything seem doable. It's indescribable how this feels to someone who's never been encouraged before.

Endearingly, Ramón often says to me that I'm a commando in special forces, just like he was. It's nutty, but it's fun. He'd say silly things like, "Fritz" (a nickname given me by father's workers when I was still a tomboy), "I'm here to help you build your empire." Then he'd get on his knees and say, "Anything you need, Fritz, I'm here. You'll be the Queen of the Empire." He's so funny and over-the-top. But, Ramón isn't just *talk*. He really *does* make it all work.

A Can-Do Guy

As noted, when I meet Ramón in early 2004 I'm mainly focused on my private counseling practice. I'd been subletting a small office in Astoria from Harvey for 1 day a week.

Having quit Harvey's operation in Kew Gardens, I'm now using this office every day, renting it directly from Ken the optometrist, for $300 a month. Soon, I'm seeing 35 to 40 patients each week in this tiny office.

Contrary to Harvey's practice experience, after awhile I have more clients in Astoria than I can handle by myself — almost 50 a week. I need to hire more therapists. But, having more therapists will require additional office space.

Ramón renovates my new office (as he later will do with the yoga studio and my home). He and his friend Fortunato build walls and put in hardwood floors. Ramón does much of it himself, while wearing Speedo underwear and listening to really loud disco music — at 2 in the morning!

I've scheduled a client for 9 AM on the day Ramón said the renovations would be finished. At sundown the day before, the offices are far from ready. But when I arrive the next morning, the whole suite looks beautiful.

From the start, everyone who comes to my new office feels comfortable and safe. The space has 3 offices for therapists, a reception area, and a waiting room. I'm still in this space today. Without Ramón, it wouldn't have happened.

Overdrive

Ramón is always running, running, running. It's partly because of his physical strength, and partly his assertive personality, that he's so driven. On the upside, this works out well when he helps me with projects. But on the downside, he's running from *himself*. He's always on the move, as if a demon is chasing him. At some point it gets tiring for everyone else, because no one can keep up with him.

I suspect he has ADHD (and I know that I do). We're *both* very driven, and we like living on the edge. We need to do extreme sports and engage in other extreme physical activities. It's almost as if otherwise we won't feel really alive.

So, I now have a buddy with whom to run for 3 or 4 miles a day, then work out at the gym, swim at the pool, go to Home Depot, remodel my apartment, do laundry, run a business. The list goes on and on. I'm considered by people who know me to be a high-energy person. I juggle work, school, and parenting 2 boys. But, Ramón has an almost supernatural level of energy. I've finally met a man who needs to be on-the-go as much as I do — yet even more so!

We'd go on "missions", as if we're Navy SEALs or Rangers in Special Forces. It's a game we play. (Today, there's no one I can go with on missions like these. I miss that.)

If we'd stayed together, we'd have accomplished still more. I wouldn't have only 1 counseling center; I'd have 3. Because Ramón would've kept encouraging me to expand. It's not that I need or want 3 counseling centers. I'm just underscoring that Ramón isn't the type who sits around and says, "Okay, the bills are paid, let's kick back, drink beer, and watch TV."

Sometimes he's too much, almost overwhelming. He always has ideas, but at times I'm exhausted. Soon, I'm seeing 45 clients and teaching 5 or 6 yoga classes a week. Yet, around 9 or 10 o'clock at night after the yoga classes are over, Ramón wants to go on some adventure, or he wants to go out to eat. There are times I say to him, "I'm really tired. You go, and I'll see you tomorrow."

Unfortunately, I have trouble turning away anyone in need, because I went without help for so long myself. So, even with a few therapists working for me, I'm soon seeing close to 50 clients a week again. Plus, I have all the extra administrative and paperwork from having several counselors working under my supervision.

And yet, my energy is nothing compared with Ramón's. Being with him is very emotionally draining, because he's so hyperactive, so intense. Then again, he's also very charming. So, most of the time I'm okay with his intensity. But, at other times, it really grows on my nerves. It's a challenging time for me.

Ramón's American Dream

After the yoga studio closes, I advise Ramón, "At this point, you should go to college." He agrees.

So I help him get accepted to my alma mater, Kingston College. I also help him with writing papers for his classes, particularly for a course in philosophy (which, after all, is rather abstract for someone new to English). A couple of times, I actually write his papers for him, even though it's not the right thing to do. But, Ramón usually gets pretty good grades on his own. And, his English keeps getting better.

To summarize what Ramón has achieved so far: In 2003, he arrives in America and starts to work as a $50 per day laborer. After meeting me, he becomes a trained yoga teacher by the end of 2004, and gets his green card in early 2005. By mid-2005, he's my partner in a yoga studio. In 2007, he's a student in good standing at Kingston College. Plus, my friend Brenda has gotten him into a construction workers union. He's now making $80,000 a year, with a 401(k), paid vacations, and medical insurance — including dental. In other words, he has achieved much of the American Dream just 4 years after getting off the plane.

As noted, I've helped and supported him in all of his accomplishments. I've introduced him to some really good people who have had his best interests at heart from the start. He could've gone really far. But, sadly, his extraordinary restless energy, and his innate aggressiveness, eventually lead to his downfall (as shall be seen).

Also in 2007, Johan is finishing college and coming back home. I need a bigger place, so I rent a 3-bedroom apartment. By this time, I'm no longer working as an escort. To reduce my expenses, I ask Ramón (who is still my friend and husband), "Why don't you help me out by renting one of my bedrooms?" He agrees to move in with me.

When I buy a house in late 2008 (while global credit markets are almost frozen), Ramón makes it possible for me to get a mortgage. I declared bankruptcy in 2006, because the yoga studio drained every penny out of my savings and my credit cards. (We'd spent about $30,000 renovating the space.) And my psychotherapy practice is not yet as successful as it will later become. So my credit is still weak.

The bank considers Ramón a better credit risk, because he has a steady union job. Although his name isn't on the deed, he assumes the risk of co-signing the bank loan for the house. I wouldn't have been able to have my own home without his help.

Once again, he's there when I need him. And, as his wife, I'm covered by his union health insurance during this period. These are some more examples of Ramón making a big difference in my life in a positive way.

So, Ramón has come a long way from walking around barefoot on the dirt floor of his childhood home, and sharing the same bed with 2 relatives. As noted, in a relatively short time he has achieved a good deal of the American Dream: A green card, enrollment in college, a steady job with good pay as well as full benefits, credit cards, etc.

On some level, we continue to have a mutually helpful relationship. But, although Ramón and I are still living together, we are growing further apart emotionally. I'm increasingly aware that he's really not well. Sadly, his self-destructive behavior results in his getting himself into an American Nightmare.

The Tangled Web

As mentioned, in February 2005 Ramón starts a job I helped him get, teaching yoga in Jackson Heights.

Later that year, Ramón gets Galina, a student of his from the Jackson Heights facility, to transfer to Astoria Hot Yoga after we open there. When I find out he's been having sex with her (she's married and has children), I tell him that I don't want her in our studio. Yet, one morning I come down from my upstairs apartment and find Galina sitting in the studio.

Another of his affairs is with Sally, a married schoolteacher that he secretly meets up with at a local bar.

Late one night when I'm already upstairs sleeping, Felicja (more about her below) calls the yoga studio. Awakened by the ringing, I pick up the phone. Felicja asks for Ramón, who is downstairs in the studio at the time because he sometimes sleeps there.

It's very hard for me to get my head around all of this. Ramón is someone that I've been assuming is gay, because of his multiple affairs with men. But, he's also trying to bed every young woman he can. And yet, he'd always deny involvement with other women. This would make me feel like *I'm* the crazy one (aka "gaslighting").

Eventually, I learn the extent of his obsession. For my own sanity, I scroll through his cellphone and examine his phone bill. He has a long list of phone numbers of women. Men too. There are also texts from many men and women.

My practical concern is that I don't want him to be inappropriate with the students at our studio. This concern is mixed in with my feelings for him — we're still life partners, even if only platonic ones by then.

Sometime in the fall of 2005, I decide to call Felicja and find out what's really going on between her and Ramón. It all comes out. She tells me he's been her boyfriend since January! He's told her he lives in Long Island City, and that he's married a *Russian* woman — only to get his green card. Actually, Felicja lives *right around the corner* from me. He'd go to her place and not come home till 4 or 5 in the morning, having me think he's been at a gay bar the whole time.

I learn from Felicja that instead he's at her house until that hour. She'd ask Ramón, "Why do you have to leave? Why don't you spend the night?"

Ramón would tell her, "I'm living with my cousin in Long Island City, and he'll be really upset if I don't come back the whole night."

As mentioned, by this time Ramón has his own car. I helped him get a driver's license by letting him practice driving my car. Once he has a license, he gets a pretty good deal on a Hyundai station wagon.

So, I'm surprised when Felicja says, "I feel so bad for him. He's driving without a license because he only has a learner's permit."

I respond, "Felicja, he has a license — why would you say he doesn't?"

She replies, "I've never seen his license — he says he doesn't have one."

I remark, "Of course he hasn't shown you his license — because then you'd see it has my address on it, which is a *short walk* from your house. He doesn't live with his cousin. He hasn't married a Russian woman, and it's not just for his green card. We were a romantic couple at the start, and we're still involved at an emotional level. So, he's lying to you about *everything*."

Felicja is in shock.

Spin Cycle

Ramón isn't in just a "triangle", because he's also with so many other men and women. For example, the studio teaches hot yoga, so there are towels that students can rent. Either Ramón or I would take the used ones to a nearby laundromat daily.

One day after putting the towels in the washing machine, he comes back to the studio and tells me he has to run somewhere (because he *always* has to run somewhere). He asks, "Do me a favor and go to the laundromat? The towels are in machines 1 and 2 — please put them in the dryer."

In between appointments with 2 different clients, I run the 2 or 3 blocks from my counseling office to the laundromat. Once there, I look at machines 1 and 2 and see there's laundry in them — but it's someone else's laundry(!) I feel like I'm in the movie *Dazed and Confused*, walking around wondering what has happened to our towels. Then a tall blonde woman with an Eastern European accent comes up to me and says, "I already put your laundry in the dryer."

I respond, "Really, why would you do that?"

She answers, "Ramón asked me to."

I think to myself, *since this schemer already had somebody else doing this for him, why did he have me come here — when I could've stayed in my office preparing for my next client?*

But this is the kind of thing Ramón would do. The woman in the laundromat is named Alexe, and she has a 7- or 8-year-old daughter. It turns out that often Ramón would spend the night at her house, and she's madly in love with him (as is Felicja).

Felicja has told me that she went to Alexe's house to confront her and tell her that *she* (Felicja) is Ramón's girlfriend, and that he's going to marry *her* — once he gets his green card and divorces "the Russian woman" (ie, *me*), whom he married just to get his papers.

After they marry (according to what he's told Felicja), they'll go to Peru, where he will buy a house for the 2 of them. Felicja has already saved $70,000 working as a nanny in Manhattan. Ramón thinks this is perfect: Her money can be the down payment, and he will fix up the house.

But, he has the same plan with me — Ramón and I have talked about buying a house in Peru and fixing it up!

During their sitdown, Alexe tells Felicja, "I don't care if he's *your* boyfriend. I'll be there for him anyway. I'm not interested in who else he's with. I don't care about that. I'm okay with him coming to my house whenever he wants. I don't ask any questions."

It's gotten really crazy. Ramón has spun a spiderweb that these women have gotten snagged in. I ask Felicja, "Do you know that he's also sleeping with men?"

Felicja replies that she's had a feeling that he is, because she knows about Flavio, the hairdresser that Ramón goes to gay bars with. I ask her, "Aren't you concerned he may be having risky sex?"

She replies, "Yes, I'm *very* concerned."

New Year's Eve

Toward the end of 2005, Ramón tells me he's going with a male friend to Atlantic City, because he needs a break from the yoga studio. Since he'll be gone for a couple of days, he'd like me to cover his classes.

First I say, "Sure, no problem."

But, I know he's lying. He's actually planning on going away with Felicja. She already told me, back when everything came out, that she and Ramón have made plans to go upstate to the Catskills, where many Polish-Americans have a big New Year's Eve party. She goes there every year.

So I tell him, "You're lying. Why don't you just tell me you're going with Felicja? I really don't care who you're going with. I'm just upset that you're lying. I wish I'd never opened the yoga studio with you, because I have to constantly cover for you and your lying. You're taking advantage of our students, and you're hiding from the women that you have unprotected sex with men. You're lying about *everything!*"

I've said to Ramón many times, "One day you're going to pay a price for all these lies, for screwing around left and right, and having all these women fall in love with you."

Ramón and I have been planning on a trip to the Cayman Islands. In the end, though, I tell him, "I'm not going. I don't want to spend my vacation with you. I don't want to go anywhere with you. I wish I could get rid of you and run the yoga studio by myself, or close it, or sell it, or something. But, I don't want you here in the studio. I'm so disgusted and done with you."

Soon Ramón sends texts and emails apologizing, and asks, "If you're not going to the Cayman Islands, can I go?"

I text him, "If you go, who are you going to take?"

He texts back, "Felicja and Flavio."

He wants to take *both* of them! I phone him and say, "That's awesome. Have you discussed this with Felicja? Will she be okay with this? — the *three* of you on an island?"

Like a 5-year-old, Ramón replies, "Uh, no, but I think it's a good idea."

I respond, "The woman is *in love* with you. Do you think she wants to share you with *Flavio?!* Felicja is a very traditional Catholic woman. She'd never go for this type of arrangement. Ramón, you're absolutely crazy!"

Fashion Statements

All his belongings, mainly clothes, are in a storage room in my basement. When I open the storage room door, there's so much stuff that his shoes fall out. I also find female socks, so I ask Ramón, "Are you serious? When you sleep with a woman you take her socks? Some men take panties — but, you're taking *socks?*"

It's a feather-in-his-cap kind of thing. But then, he also takes *men's* socks. There are times when he brings back cashmere socks. Apparently, some of the men he goes out with have money. He sometimes wears regular white socks like the ones sold at Footlocker priced at 3 for $10, but at other times Ramón wears fancy men's socks. At still other times, he wears red-and-blue-striped women's socks. Or, he might come home wearing a woman's pink Gucci baseball cap. (Maybe it's partly his way of remembering who's who.)

Eventually, Ramón starts bringing home designer clothing, like Armani wear. He says he met a Russian girl who works as a high-end escort, and she takes him shopping. He accumulates whole collections of new clothes. Since Ramón lies about so many things, it might actually be a wealthy businessman. (I no longer trust anything he says.)

So now, he's wearing Armani jeans, shirts, and belts that he's getting from one (or more) of his new lovers. And yet, he's still sleeping with Felicja and Alexe.

Parallel Lives

One day Ramón comes to the studio with a whole car trunk full of plants. He asks me if I'd watch them for Eléna (a woman I hadn't known about), because she's going to Greece for the summer and needs someone to care for them. I say, "Fine — put them in the backyard next to my plants."

So, there is Felicja, Alexe, and now *Eléna* — whose plants I'm taking care of(!)

Another time, Ramón shows up with Ed, a gay friend in his 60's. Ed is accompanied by Cody, a young man who is Ed's lover and live-in "servant". Ramón tells me what a great guy Ed is, what a sweetheart, such a wonderful guy — and says we should go out to dinner with Ed and Cody.

I'm totally not in the mood to go out to dinner with these 3 clowns. And, I'm sad and angry that Ramón is telling so many lies to so many people, potentially putting all of them at great health risk.

Mixed Feelings

I'm also upset because Astoria Hot Yoga could've done well if it were run by a person with integrity — instead of someone who violates boundaries left and right. And yet, I can't be completely mad at Ramón, because there are many times I've needed his help, and he's always been there for me. When I need something fixed, he comes and fixes it. Because he's so handy and reliable, I decide to remain his platonic friend, in spite of his flaws.

Still, I feel if we were really friends, he wouldn't lie so much and keep all these secrets from me. He's said that I'm like an older sister, that we're family and we'll always be there for each other. But I respond, "I really can't feel that way about you because every time you lie to me, I feel very hurt. I can't trust you, since you lie so much."

His antics are increasingly getting on my nerves. The many incidents, the multiple relationships, the parallel lives, all the lies. I've never met anybody who with a straight face and a smile could say to me how important I am in his life, though he's lying about all the things that are really important to *him*. Does anyone actually mean anything to him? Or, are we all just means to an end — to get him what he wants? And so, our relationship steadily deteriorates.

Early Warnings

Then I learn that Roxanna, a Venezuelan woman, has sent Ramón a very emotional email saying she never wants to hear from him again, and that she wishes he'd die, because he has hurt her so much that she will never forgive him.

I say to him, "You see what's happening? Women are enraged by your lying to them. You need to really think about your part in this. You don't seem to see anything wrong with what you're doing."

I warn him not just once, but over and over, "Ramón, you're going too far. You're going to pay a high price, because one day somebody is going to push back. I don't know what's going to happen, but *something* has to give. It's better to stop *before* things get completely out of control."

Yet he doesn't listen, so things continue sliding downhill for us. It becomes harder and harder for me to be around him. I could've tolerated a lot of things if he were honest with me. I think his being honest would've really helped us *both*. But, sadly, I don't think he's ever been honest in his life.

Towaway Zone

One night I get very angry at Ramón, because though he told me he isn't seeing Felicja anymore, I see his car parked in front of her house when I drive by. I have a set of keys for his Hyundai, along with having my own Jeep. I call a friend and ask her if she'd be my partner-in-crime — by driving my Jeep back to my house — if I "steal" Ramón's Hyundai, and take it over to my place?

She's like, "Sure — no problem."

I want to teach Ramón a lesson — to have him wake up in the morning, not find his car, and think it's stolen. My friend is a really good sport about it. For us girls, this "car caper" is a fun adventure!

Ramón calls me in the morning, "Did you take my car?"

I answer, "No, why would you think I took your car?"

He says, "Because it's not here anymore."

I say, "Maybe it's stolen. Or maybe you have so many tickets that it's been towed to the car pound. I have no idea. Where was it parked?"

He answers, "It doesn't matter."

Later that morning, he takes a taxi to the yoga studio and sees that his car is there. I say to him, "You see? This is what happens when you lie to people — they get mad and do crazy things. Your car is right here — someone dropped it off. Figure it out."

He laughs — and then we both laugh about it together.

There are quite a few situations where I want to seek revenge, to get back at him in some way. But, I could never really hurt him, because I realize the whole thing is so silly and crazy. Although I'd do little things like this, I never do him any real harm.

But, I'm definitely angered by his behavior. I'm not mad because he's sleeping with other women. I'm upset because he's my best friend, someone that in many ways I greatly admire, who makes me feel proud that he cares for me and supports me. But, by the same token, that someone whom I've allowed into my life can *lie* to me the way he does — that's what angers me so.

I read the emails that Felicja sends him. (By this time, I know his password.) She writes to him that she's breaking up with him — but not because he's bisexual. She can accept that. Instead, she's leaving him because he's a liar.

I feel the same way. I'm not upset because he's bi, but because he lies so much. The betrayal is what's so hurtful.

Violating My Psychotherapy Client

One of my counseling clients, Amy, also becomes a yoga student of ours. She's 34 or 35 — close to Ramón's age — and married with 3 young boys. One day in a counseling session she asks me, "What's the deal with Ramón?"

I reply, "What do you mean?"

Amy answers, "He kissed me in the hallway after yoga class, and I just want your opinion: Should I go for it?"

I'm devastated. It's really disturbing for me as a therapist to hear that my husband — who, in spite of all the betrayals, I've believed is my best friend — has just now kissed one of my counseling clients!

First of all, this is a tremendous violation of boundaries, because a teacher, like a therapist, is in a position of authority. There's a power differential. A student looks up to a teacher. A student is entitled to be safe from the solicitation of romantic or erotic favors of any kind. Kissing a client or student is absolutely inappropriate.

So, now I'm furious at Ramón. This is *my* business too, and he's ruining it. I also feel very hurt.

And, it isn't just Amy. Ramón is very affectionate with the attractive men too, often hugging and kissing them.

One yoga student, who is openly gay, asks me if Ramón is gay too. I answer him, "I really don't know." I didn't answer the question candidly, because if Ramón's not open about it, I'm not going to gratuitously "out" him.

And yet, for her safety, I do say to Amy, "I think you should be very careful with him because he dates both women and men, and he's very promiscuous."

Her revelation that Ramón has kissed her comes as such a shock that I'm too angry and upset to handle her question as well as I should have. However, I feel Amy *needs* to know, since she has a husband who shouldn't be put at risk. Ramón could have one or more STD's. I never caught anything from him, but my suspicion that he doesn't use protection with his other partners will later be confirmed. Further, Amy's my counseling client, adding to my duty to warn her.

Crime and Punishment

Because of his forceful nature, Ramón won't take *no* for an answer. For example, if he wants to bring over a piece of furniture he's found, even if I say *no* he brings it over anyway. Far worse, it seems that if a woman says *no* to having sex, *that doesn't stop him either.*

In 2008, while we are still married, I get an early morning call from Ramón telling me he's in the Tombs (the local jail in Manhattan). According to his version, the night before he left a club with a woman. They were both drunk and hopped into a taxi together. He adds that in the car she was hot and heavy for him, kissing him and more.

But, when they arrived at her apartment on Park Avenue, and he followed her up to her door, she tried to close it on him. He pushed his way in, and asked for a glass of wine or, if not that, water. She told him, "If you don't leave, I'll call the police."

He still didn't leave, so then she did call the police. When NYPD arrived, Ramón was still in the building lobby.

Although he was charged with forceful entry into her apartment, the charge was later dismissed. (I see this episode as a caution light, but nothing more.)

Caught on Camera

At least 1 night a week, Ramón goes to a downtown Manhattan club that's his favorite. He's a regular, so the doormen always let him in. Many pretty models go there, and in the recent past some of them met a bad end soon after leaving. In addition to the tragic consequences for the women and their families, there's been other bad publicity for the club. As a result, the owners have installed video cameras everywhere.

In March 2009, Ramón meets Olivia, a 24-year-old model, while they're at the club. As the evening wears on, Olivia gets falling-down drunk. Eventually, Ramón takes her to the apartment he and I had in Astoria (by then I've moved into my private home). While there, they have sex. Because she's originally from Scandinavia and hasn't lived long in Manhattan, she's never been to Astoria, Queens. So when she wakes up the next day, she doesn't know where she is.

The 2 of them go to breakfast at Starbucks, where Ramón takes her picture. He then drives Olivia back to Manhattan, and drops her off at her apartment on the Upper East Side. (So, they both seem to be unaware that there's a problem.)

Meanwhile, her roommate is concerned because they'd gone to the club together, and then Olivia seemed to disappear, leaving behind her coat and her pocketbook (which implies she was too drunk to consent to anything). Her roommate is understandably worried, and calls the police.

Once Olivia gets home, her roommate encourages her to go to a nearby hospital. A test is done that's positive for semen. And, her sample matches samples found in 2 other women who had filed similar complaints — one in 2008, and another in 2007. Now there are 3 DNA samples that match. (So, Ramón has indeed been having unsafe sex with multiple partners, as I've suspected all along.)

By June, the police and the prosecutor have put the whole case together. They have no problem finding Ramón, because when he dropped Olivia off back in March, he gave her his phone number and invited her to call him to get together again. Instead, detectives call and ask him his full name and where he lives. While on the phone, he admits everything he did with Olivia (because he still doesn't realize he has done something terribly wrong).

Detectives go to the Astoria apartment and arrest him. Even so, he doesn't realize it's a big deal. None of the women accused him of violence or threats of violence, so he thinks he's in the clear. (By then I've known Ramón intimately for 5 years, and as far as I know, Ramón has never been violent, or even physically intimidating, with anyone.

Of course, it *is* a big deal. What he's done is wrong — *very wrong*. But, perhaps because of his background from rural Peru, and his own history of being abused, he doesn't realize that his actions are completely unacceptable. So, he naively makes self-incriminating statements to the police, without even thinking to contact a lawyer.

Ramón is charged with kidnapping (because he took Olivia from Manhattan to Queens while she was barely conscious), as well as rape. The club's security cameras recorded what happened there. The playback shows Ramón trying to help her walk. When she falls on the floor, he picks her up like a sack of potatoes, and carries her out of the club. Seeing the video, I can't believe my eyes. I think, *Oh my God!*

Together with some of his family members, I help him raise $10,000 to hire a lawyer — now that he's already admitted everything(!)

I realize there's nothing more I can do for him. He has to learn this lesson on his own. As the saying goes, *You have to hit bottom*. Having decided to sever all ties, I file for divorce.

The divorce is finalized shortly before Ramón goes to prison in October 2009, after entering into a plea agreement for the kidnapping and statutory rape of Olivia. He's sentenced to 3½ years in prison, to be followed by deportation back to Peru.

Already, he has another girlfriend, Esmeralda. She plans on waiting until he's out of prison, then going with him to Peru. I sense that Ramón doesn't want me to be involved, so I stay out of it.

I don't visit him in prison because it's all so sad. Ramón is a good person in so many ways. But in retrospect, I realize that he had a predatory side. His crime wasn't only one night of drunken madness. Over a period of years, he went looking for young women to prey on — women who were too drunk to be capable of meaningfully consenting to sex. (We'll never know how many didn't come forward.)

I wasn't aware of this side of Ramón's nature until his arrest. I feel very disillusioned by the whole experience. I've lost a close friend and a dependable partner. Ramón was a very important person in my life, but there's no happy ending for our relationship.

After the Fall

While in prison, Ramón sends me a number of letters (and I reply to some of them). He also sends a bracelet he made for me, in the color of the Peruvian Special Forces — yellow and black. It's inscribed "Fritz". He wants me to always remember that I'm a "commando" in Special Forces.

Ramón is released from prison in October 2012, because 6 months for good behavior were deducted from his 3½-year sentence. I haven't heard from him in some time. I still wear the bracelet he made when I run in races. He's the one who really got my warrior spirit going. I've become so much stronger physically because of the intensity of the workouts he got me started on.

Even though I'm now over 60, I feel stronger than when I was 30. I can lift more than many of the younger girls at the gym. I never imagined that I could do the things I do now — like bench-press 100 pounds. After Ramón went to prison, I started pushing myself even harder, sort of in his memory. I feel very sad that he went to prison (even though I know he deserved it).

Reflections

I suspected early on that I'd never have real emotional intimacy with Ramón. This hurt a lot. And, his constantly acting out sexually — with both men and women — also hurt a lot.

But, often we hope that we can work through certain difficulties in a relationship. We feel if we are patient, the problems will be resolved down the road. In the very beginning of our marriage, I did think things would work out — that we'd eventually achieve real intimacy. But, learning about his compulsive sexual behavior over time — seemingly with anyone and everyone — eventually destroyed my hope.

As far back as 2005, I was feeling a lot of sadness because of Ramón's cheating. Plus, his betrayals brought back my feelings of having been abandoned by my mother. So, in a sense, I was mourning both losses at the same time.

And yet, being involved with Ramón was a catalyst for me to process a lot of my pain from childhood. In a way, it was a good thing, because it's part of the therapeutic process to confront the wounds from our past in order to be able to live truly authentic lives. If we don't mourn our past, we're going to be stuck in it.

I myself was emotionally stuck from the time mother left. At that age, I couldn't process my hurt and confusion. I started using heroin at age 14 to avoid my underlying feelings about being abandoned by her and abused by father.

At age 19, I gave birth to Lucas, as another way to avoid my real issues. A few years later I had Johan. So, my focus on was on both of *them* — instead of *my* unresolved issues. I got off drugs for a time, but when father started wasting away from a failing liver, I began to use again. After father died, my drug use really took off. Only when I got off heroin for good did my healing process begin. It happened bit by bit (and I still sometimes avoid dealing with certain losses).

Unlike my childhood experiences, though, I wasn't a helpless victim in my relationship with Ramón. Instead, part of me was living out a fantasy that he'd change — even though all the evidence pointed in the opposite direction. Yet, the realistic part of me knew that it could never work. For months and months (perhaps 2 years in total), I often cried in the evening, because I felt such tremendous loss.

In sum, my marriage to Ramón was in a way therapeutic. But he broke my heart.

𝕎orking 9-5

Earlier I mentioned having had a good internship while at Uptown University. I think this internship made earning their Master's degree in Social Work worthwhile.

The 3 areas I could choose from are the clinical track, the research track, or the administrative track. I pick the clinical track, which is divided into 5 different specialties: Mental Health, which entails working in a psychiatric hospital; Children and the Family, which would mean working for a foster care agency (like Manhattan Family Hospital); Early Childhood Intervention, which includes family intervention, like NYC Administrative Childhood Services; the World of Work, covering Employee Assistance Programs (EAP's); and a track focused on drug and alcohol abuse, which requires interning in one of NYC's substance abuse facilities.

I've already had enough experience with substance abuse in my own life. After years of NA and AA, I don't feel the need to learn more about addicts and alcoholics. And, I've worked for 5 years at Manhattan Family. There I learned a good deal about troubled families, and the socioeconomic differences between the South Bronx, Harlem, and other low-income neighborhoods — versus Fifth Avenue, Soho, and Tribeca, where the quality of life is so different.

In New York City, some are leading lives of privilege, while many are surviving in dire poverty, with lots of abuse in their life, along with other depressing issues. Having spent a number of years in poverty myself, I'm not yet ready to re-immerse myself in those issues.

Anthony's Secret Life

So, I choose the Employee Assistance Program. My internship is at WellWorx, an EAP where companies send workers in need of special help. My supervisors are April and Marisa, and my co-intern is Anthony, who lives with his parents on Staten Island.

Anthony's mother knows he's gay. His father (already disappointed that Anthony isn't following his footsteps as a well-paid mason) either doesn't know, or pretends not to know. So, Anthony's openly gay while in Manhattan, but returns to the closet when he goes home to Staten Island.

Besides being very caring, Anthony is quite smart. He receives his Master's degree from Uptown U when he's only 24 (I'm 41 by then). In spite of our age difference, we've remained friends. Sixteen years later, Anthony, April, Marisa, and I still go out to dinner 3 or 4 times a year.

April: Not the Hippie Type

April isn't a stereotypical social worker in a muu muu and sandals. She married an anesthesiologist, so they are financially well off. They spend 3 or 4 months a year in Italy, then travel elsewhere, for example the Middle East.

April is a good supervisor, and she provides me with excellent clinical experience. She sees to it that I work with a range of people, from manual laborers and uniformed government workers to big shots at banks and law firms. (She has a lot of contacts in the 2nd category.)

For example, I accompany her on presentations she delivers at companies where there's been a suicide or other sudden death of an employee. She makes a point of introducing me to important people at these companies.

This is my daytime work in 2000. In the evening and on weekends, I'm still supporting myself (and helping my sons pay for college) by escorting clients I meet through my website. Often during the daytime, I'd set up an escorting appointment for the evening hours. One day Anthony says to me, "What are you doing on the computer when you seem so intently focused?"

I don't tell him at the time. But years later over dinner, I reveal what had really gone on. He remarks, "I had a feeling, because there was something so *secretive* about you!"

In sum, the internship at WellWorx is a good experience, because I'm working with all kinds of high functioning clients, and dealing with many different issues.

Twin Towers

In late 2001, April calls me and asks, "Do you want a job as a consultant helping employees deal with ongoing stress from 9/11? It's at NYBank, and the pay is $100 an hour." Of course, I take the job.

World Trade Center, September 2001

These employees were at NYBank's headquarters when the nearby Twin Towers were destroyed. The resulting shock wave caused their building's exterior wall of glass to collapse. One of their co-workers died from the falling debris.

Many bank employees are traumatized by the whole episode. NYBank's management is bringing back a few employees at a time — about 100 people every 2 weeks.

Though I'm not there for very long — maybe 6 weeks — this brief stint changes my whole outlook. It gives me the sense that there's finally a way for me to earn my way out of poverty *legally*, a hope I hadn't really felt until this point.

At Manhattan Family, once a year they gave each of us a nice heart-shaped pin, signifying that social workers have heart. Many of the staff are nuns and their expenses are low. A heart-shaped pin makes a fine token of appreciation for them.

But, I'm not a nun. I'm just an ordinary survivor of a dysfunctional upbringing. If you have 2 kids in your household (for a time I have 4), you can't make ends meet in NYC on $27,000 a year (much less the $22,000 a year I made when I started). I tried, but I couldn't do it.

I'm glad I choose an EAP internship. This way, I won't get stuck in some dysfunctional bureaucracy, like Manhattan Family, where little gets done besides shuffling paper from one desk to the next. In such workplaces, clients get relatively little help, because so much of the professional staff's time is spent doing tedious paperwork (which I suspect no one ever reads). Social workers burn out at such jobs.

Most clients in an EAP are fine with needing short-term help for one specific problem. Whereas clients whose multiple issues keep them trapped in social service bureaucracies for years on end would rather not be there at all. The professionals and support staff, frustrated by overwork and the inability to actually help people who are burdened with so many issues, don't want to be there either. Plus, professionals and support staff alike are paid so poorly that they lack even a financial motive for doing a good job. It feels like a constant losing battle for both clients and staff.

By contrast, working under April's supervision makes me realize that there are a lot of things a social worker can do that are both emotionally and financially rewarding.

Helping Others Recover

Therapists study various textbook theories while in school and afterwards. But I think they draw their deepest insights from their personal experiences. For that reason, I think my strength is working with people who've been traumatized, particularly during their childhood years. I can pick up on early-life trauma in a client almost immediately.

Conversely, I'm not as adept with clients who have little or no recollection of past hurts. For example, a client comes in with symptoms of Obsession Compulsion Disorder (OCD). Yet, they report that otherwise everything in their life is fine: Their childhood was great, their parents got along well, nothing has ever really bothered them, and they have little in the way of early memories.

And yet, they're washing their hands 10 times a day, sometimes more. They feel an urgent need to wash before doing the laundry, after doing the laundry, each time they fold a shirt, each time they put a shirt in the drawer. But, they can't make any connections to why this might be happening. I have a hard time helping such a client.

These days, OCD and severe anxiety are being treated mainly with medication. I do believe that medication is appropriate at times, although often I fear that referring a client to a psychiatrist for medication is an easy way out for both the client and me. Still, a lot of people would rather take medication than explore where their anxiety may be coming from. Though it's frustrating for me as a therapist, many people don't want to look at what's going on inside.

Also, I've come to realize that I'm running a business. I have many bills to pay, including paychecks for the counselors working for me. If someone feels better just by coming week after week to talk about surface issues as they arise, without going any deeper, I can do that. But, it's not really satisfying to work with a person who has no interest in gaining awareness, making connections, and reintegrating that which was fragmented in their past.

The 3 "S"s

In a nutshell, my goal is for each client to gain 3 things: self-awareness, self-expression, and self-possession.

This includes learning how to verbally express needs: physical needs, emotional needs, spiritual needs, whatever needs ought to be communicated to others. Expressed needs will not always be met. But at least someone can learn how to appropriately put them into words. Many people don't know how to do this, though they feel they're being violated in one way or another, so they wind up silently hurt and angry.

I also work well with clients who have in some way been close to the events of 9/11, or have been affected by a natural disaster, for example an earthquake or a hurricane.

The Dark Tunnel

But, as mentioned, I do best with people who had ongoing early childhood trauma, and who are willing to walk along a painful path. It's like entering a tunnel, walking through, and then coming out the other side with a profound shift.

Most children are very resilient, as we all know. They almost always manage to function on a day-to-day basis. They go to school, and have certain other responsibilities in getting through the day. Plus, they also have to be *children*.

But, a child's psyche can handle only so much trauma. If a child experiences too much, they push much of it into the background in order to survive. Often when they reach adolescence, the traumatic material they couldn't deal with earlier returns to the foreground, manifesting itself in various symptoms.

This is one reason why some adolescents can be so difficult. In addition to the changes hormones bring about at the physical and emotional level, the unresolved early issues emerge. It's no wonder that these adolescents start drinking, using drugs, and acting out in other ways. A few even start to cut themselves. In general, they take high risks.

Of course, some risk-taking is normal for adolescents. But,

it's not normal for healthy adolescents to cut themselves even a little, much less to mutilate themselves. Or binge drink, inject substances into their arm, smoke meth, abuse opioids, or heaven knows what else — resulting in evermore admittances to hospital ER's. So, though some acting out is normal, people who have been traumatized as children often exhibit really self-destructive behavior in adolescence.

Unfortunately, some clients are so damaged that I can't do very much to help them. As a clinician, and an empathetic human being, this makes me very sad. I try my best, but sometimes I have to accept that this is as good as it gets for a particular client. Not everyone has the strength to go through that dark tunnel I mentioned before.

A Road Less Traveled

I believe we're born whole. But afterward, to one extent or another, many of us are emotionally injured during childhood. I'm not blaming anybody — not parents, teachers, government, or society generally. But, regardless of external circumstances, I believe that the human condition inevitably contains a certain amount of suffering.

As noted, many people take various prescribed anti-anxiety medications to deal with their issues, partly because insurers prefer the illusion that the body, rather than the psyche, is what needs healing. Instead, I accompany a client along a road less traveled. We stop at various mileposts from their childhood, examining what has injured them, and looking at what defenses they have developed to protect themselves against further wounding.

Once we investigate and understand *what* has wounded them, we can begin to work on those 3 S's: self-awareness, self-expression, and ultimately, self-possession. At the end of our journey, the client can be whole again.

Choosing To Be Whole

But, although pain is inevitable, I think in therapy we can discover that the degree of suffering is largely a choice (which is also a lesson of 12-Step programs). Once someone learns that happiness and suffering are mainly choices, they can largely liberate themselves from suffering.

Before we can exercise the choice to reduce our suffering, though, we must 1st have awareness that change is necessary. But what specifically creates awareness that we must change? Some people feel it's a matter of divine intervention. Suddenly a person looks at their life and has a spiritual awakening: *I'm sick and tired of being sick and tired. I've made such a mess out of my life! How can I change it?*

Sometimes they just put 2 plus 2 together, and conclude that they have to give up something (or certain feelings or behaviors) they thought they couldn't live without.

As noted, my own life experiences have helped me recognize trauma and post-traumatic stress in a new client. This aids me in determining which clients I can best assist in getting through the tunnel to the other side, versus those whose current situation is likely to be as good as it gets.

Even so, I'm still supportive of those in the 2nd group. I empathize and sympathize with them, as a hand-holding partner. Unfortunately, some people do not get much better. They remain stuck in their anxieties and other symptoms. And, even more sadly, a few just continue to act out self-destructive patterns.

Sex Addiction

The reason the adult-companionship industry exists at all is pretty simple: A man feels lonely and is willing to pay for someone who agrees to help his loneliness go away (even if only briefly). But, what for many is an occasional episode of escapism becomes for some a compulsion that interferes with everyday life. In other words, an addiction. A lot of the time, addiction is acting out in order to meet some need that was not met at an earlier time in life. There's a kind of desperation about addictions, like a child trying to escape when having a bad dream.

Awhile back, I have a psychotherapy client in his early 40's who loves his girlfriend. They're engaged to marry, but they aren't sleeping together. This is perfectly normal for many couples. But in this case, he's on the internet having cyber-sex with women all over the country. (Naturally, without his fiancée's knowledge.)

Sometimes he meets one of these women in person. For example, he flew to Texas and paid a 19-year-old local girl to spend a weekend with him.

Although he had an exciting time with her, his obsession is causing him increasing anxiety. He fears the woman he loves will leave him. She has started questioning him, "We're getting married — why won't you sleep with me?"

In session, he tells me he wants to work on this, and learn the *why* of it all. But as things evolve, he realizes he doesn't want to give up his addiction to internet porn and cybersex. After several sessions, I tell him, "There's no point in your coming to therapy. You're not ready yet. Even though these activities are causing pain, they're also giving you pleasure. Because you're not willing to let them go, there's no benefit for you to continue seeing me. Whenever you're ready to actually work on this, you can call me and we can resume.

Another Child of the Holocaust

Lilly was born in Sweden in 1958. Her parents emigrated there after their liberation from Auschwitz at the end of WW II. They came to the US in 1961.

Lilly is a bit of a "character" when I meet her in 2003. She has been in counseling, on and off, for years. But, no other therapist has wanted to see her for an extended period. I work with Lilly right up to the end, and grow very fond of her along the way.

When I meet her, she has just gotten married to Arthur, a social worker who, like Lilly, is an adult child of Holocaust survivors. (They met in a children of Holocaust survivors support group.)

Lilly has one sibling, a medical doctor. He's the pride and joy of their parents. By contrast, Lilly hasn't been capable of keeping a job — any job. She's not attentive to her appearance, and walks about the neighborhood in a long coat over clothes that never match. Because they view her as an oddball, no one in her family takes her seriously. Yet in spite of this, plus her being overweight, she is still an attractive woman in my eyes.

One day, while I'm out of my office around lunchtime, I see Lilly talking away to a police officer. She'd strike up a conversation with perfect strangers (uncommon in a big city), because she has such a strong unmet need to feel connected, to be heard.

In therapy, she reports that neither of her parents are present for her. Her father suffers from chronic depression. Her mother is very anxious, overbearing, and controlling. Since they married, every time she and Arthur visit her parents, her mother gives them bags and bags of groceries.

Prisoners at Auschwitz were severely underfed, so perhaps her mother is compensating for her past trauma by always trying to overfeed Lilly. But, whatever her mother's reason, Lilly can't stand this. In general, she finds it extremely difficult to cope with her parents.

A "Hopeless Case"

When Lilly first comes to me, she is already pretty well known in the local therapeutic community. As noted, a number of therapists have refused to continue seeing her. They felt she couldn't be helped, so they weren't going to invest much of themselves in her treatment. When she's referred to me, I'm basically told she's a hopeless case. (I'm even advised to not take her too seriously.)

For a long while, I too find it trying to sit and listen to Lilly. But I force myself to be there for her with love and compassion, in order to establish *some* degree of rapport. Lilly's depression manifests itself by her talking nonstop — about nothing of any consequence. Her words go in circles for a bit, then suddenly lurch off on some tangent. Before long, I feel drained of energy just trying to follow what she is saying. Yet, I sense that I have to accept this until Lilly feels safe enough to open up to me.

Because I refuse to give up on her, a number of months pass in this way. Finally I say, "Lilly, every time we have a session, I feel like I'm zoning out. I actually get exhausted. I'm wondering if this happens between you and other people?"

Lilly laughs loudly, and says, "It happens all the time! People totally tune me out, and walk away. Others just ignore me completely, because they think I'm *crazy*."

To my surprise, this exchange profoundly shifts our whole relationship. Suddenly, Lilly starts talking about the things that really matter to her. We've had a breakthrough, and are finally beginning real therapy.

No one has ever *really* listened to Lilly. I think her parents are still so traumatized by Auschwitz that they aren't ever able to hear her and take her problems seriously.

Her physician brother would verbally abuse Lilly, because she's a cigarette smoker. He'd say to her things like, "You're going to die from lung cancer if you don't stop smoking." Or, "If you don't quit smoking, I'll stop talking to you." At some point, he actually *does* stop talking to her.

This is very upsetting to Lilly, but eventually she evolves to be able say, "He's my brother. I love him. But, I don't deserve to be treated like this just because I smoke cigarettes. It's not a reason for him to stop talking to me." This is one of the signs that Lilly has started to be a little bit more assertive. Still, it's a very slow process.

Beginning to Blossom

Lilly is intelligent, and she has a 4-year college degree. But although she's worked at various temporary assignments, in the past she wasn't able to hold down a long-term job. So, I'm happy that while she's seeing me, she gets a regular job, working at a group home for developmentally-delayed children — another sign that she's making some progress.

As part of her job, she accompanies one of the boys to and from school and his other activities. Unfortunately, there are occasions when he's very mean. One time he breaks her glasses. Another time he punches her.

But, in spite of setbacks, Lilly begins to blossom. Little by little, I can see that she's developing real relationships with people — not just talking at them until they walk away from her. At work, she starts to express her own views at team meetings. In session, we talk about how much she enjoys her job. I'm really happy for her, because she's finally finding meaning in her life.

When she's eventually assigned to a different child, she has to say goodbye to the boy she's been helping. In spite of his occasional abuse, she's sad their relationship is ending. This is real stuff that we're now talking about, real feelings.

In what turns out to be our last session (though we don't realize it at the time), we discuss the purpose of life. Lilly now realizes that it doesn't matter whether she's a doctor, a lawyer, a homemaker, or whatever field she works in. What counts isn't her social status, nor her educational attainment, nor what she does *per se*.

Rather, it's how she does her work, how *connected* she is to it. Does her work fill a void? Does it make her feel like she's having a meaningful life? As things have turned out, Lilly has found her purpose by working with children who have special needs.

The Last Session

After this session, I never see Lilly again — while she's still conscious. Though we do schedule another meeting, on the day of the appointment Lilly calls to cancel. She's at Mount Lebanon Hospital, awaiting the results of a physical exam. The doctors have found a spot on one of her lungs, and she's being admitted as an in-patient because of their concern that it might be cancerous.

It all happens so quickly. A biopsy reveals that Lilly has Stage IV lung cancer, meaning it has already spread to other parts of her body. So, it's inoperable.

Arthur calls to tell me that the doctors haven't given Lilly much time to live — perhaps as little as one month. I'm shocked and saddened, especially because Lilly was just starting to really find herself.

I've worked with Lilly throughout her transformation. I've seen her change from a person who is so desperate to connect with people that she pushes them away, to become instead someone who is a joy to sit with and engage in meaningful conversation.

Although Lilly has already undergone a huge change, I feel that this might have been just the beginning, that perhaps she could've grown much more. It seems as if the minute she found herself and started to enjoy life, she was diagnosed with incurable cancer.

Lilly manages to hang onto life another 8 months, all spent in the hospital. At some point, Arthur calls and tells me, "It would mean a lot to Lilly if you could visit her. She speaks often about you. She says you are the best therapist she's ever had, and that her sessions with you have really meant a lot to her." (I didn't know that she feels that way until this moment.)

I visit Lilly in the hospital a few times. By now, she just lies in bed unconscious. She couldn't have really talked to me even if she were conscious, because she's attached to tubes for eating and breathing. Not that long ago, she was increasingly in control of her life. Now she's completely helpless.

While there, I meet her parents and her brother. Although Lilly is unconscious, her mother keeps saying, "Lilly, wake up, wake up. You have to eat, Lilly, wake up." After awhile, the nurses take her mother away, explaining, "You need to let her rest."

Her brother exclaims, in an elevated voice, "I *told* her not to smoke! Why did she smoke?! Why didn't she listen to me?" Her father remains silent.

Feeling Lilly's Presence

Late one night, I suddenly awaken from my sleep, thinking of Lilly. I feel very anxious for her. I'm not a religious person in a conventional way, but I sense her spirit in the room with me. When morning comes, Arthur calls and tells me Lilly died overnight.

I attend the Orthodox Jewish funeral service for Lilly. We're the same age, and now that she's gone, I feel very sad.

Interestingly, Lilly liked the fact that I'm of German and Austrian ancestry. Of course, I didn't go into any of the details about my background, like what father did during the war, or how he raised me. (Therapists rarely disclose details of their background and personal life to a client. But, of course, I couldn't hide my German accent.)

Unfortunately, it was part of Lilly's journey to only get a taste of a different life before the end, to liberate herself from her past, and the damage that her parents had unwittingly done to her. They obviously are good people, but they were traumatized by Auschwitz. Often people who are traumatized cannot be really present for someone else, because they're too preoccupied with daily survival. Psychologically, Lilly's parents are still basically just surviving from day to day, as they were during the war.

Lilly was able to undo some of the damage this caused her, to become present for others, while also acknowledging her own needs. Given how long she had been stuck in the same place, this was major progress.

As she got older, no one thought Lilly would ever marry. She unexpectedly found love in her early 40's, when she married Arthur.

I've often thought about Lilly since then. I feel honored to have had the privilege of working with her.

Some Are More Fragile Than Others

Not everyone who struggles has had their life altered by a catastrophe like WW II. People with ordinary lives may also have severe problems dealing with everyday issues.

Greta was referred to me by another therapist in 2003, and has been a client of mine ever since. As with Lilly, at the time of referral I'm told to just do my best — that there isn't much hope for Greta, who by then is in her late 50's.

Greta presents with a long history of severe anxiety and panic attacks. She has already been in therapy for over a decade. When I meet her, she's very guarded. She doesn't want to talk about her childhood, or anything else in her past. She only wants to talk about her husband, Steve, and their troubled marriage.

Steve is addicted to watching porn on cable tv, and they're no longer physically intimate. In fact, throughout the marriage, they've had little physical intimacy.

Steve watches porn every night. When Greta complains, he tells her to go to sleep. She hates this, and would say to him, "Don't tell me when to go to sleep." He'd respond, "You're being stupid, Greta. Shut up and go to sleep."

This is an argument they have almost every night.

An Unwanted Child

In spite of her initial reticence to talk about her past, after a number of sessions Greta reveals that she does have a history of childhood struggles. When she was a baby, her birth mother was unable to care for her. A woman who owned a hair salon, and was unable to have children of her own, adopted Greta. When growing up, Greta never felt loved or wanted. She always felt like a burden on everyone else.

When she was 9, the family cat jumped onto her face and scratched her right eye. Her adoptive mother didn't take her to a hospital. Instead, even though this poor child was in pain from an eye injury, she was scolded and told to go to bed (as now happens with Steve).

A few days later, still complaining that she couldn't see out of her injured eye, Greta was taken to an eye doctor. He said there was no longer much that could be done. If she'd been brought to him right away, her sight in that eye might have been saved. But now it was too late.

Yet subsequently, her mother and grandmother sometimes made remarks about her eye (which was now permanently disfigured) as if it were *Greta's* fault that the cat scratched her, and that she wasn't given timely medical attention. (I don't know if they consciously intended to blame Greta, but this is how Greta felt when she was growing up.)

Also in her youth, Greta was sexually abused by an adult male relative who from time to time visited her home. Although there was no penetration, he had her sit on his lap, and then molested her by touching her private parts.

Sadly, as a child (and even well into adulthood), Greta was never able to speak up for herself. She has always been wary of other people.

Until her mother got home from working at the beauty parlor, Greta had to go after school to the nearby home of her mother's friend, Wande. Though Greta is intelligent, she had some learning difficulties. So, besides her babysitting role, Wande also helped Greta with her homework.

My sense is that Wande was an alcoholic at the time. In any event, she was mean and abusive to Greta, yelling at her every day, and forcing her to write things over and over. Greta has really painful memories of this.

In addition, Greta's adoptive father, a truck driver, was killed in a vehicular accident when she was only 10.

We Begin Therapy

At the outset, Greta reports that she always feels like she's not really herself. She has difficulty speaking with people, and when she does speak to them, she takes on their personality. If someone else is laughing, Greta laughs too. If someone else says, "It's a nice day", Greta automatically responds, "Yeah, it's a nice day."

Many people are agreeable in this way because they choose to be. With Greta, it isn't a choice. She really doesn't know if she has an opinion of her own. If she's important. If she has a right to speak. If she exists at all. She constantly wonders if what she's saying is "okay". She weighs every word carefully before she says it. She worries whether she's saying the right thing, the wrong thing, whether she should be quiet or speak up.

She's internally preoccupied in general. There's some mild delusional thinking, but she isn't psychotic. For example, sometimes in New York City (anywhere actually, but in a big city especially), someone on a train or bus acts very oddly. When this happens in Greta's presence, she anxiously wonders if *she's* to blame for this person's strange behavior.

To be sure, Greta is a good soul who has raised a son and daughter who are now responsible adults. So, she's not without solid accomplishment in life.

Anonymous Donor

Because Steve was unable to provide her with children, Greta became pregnant via a sperm bank. This was one of the few occasions when Greta took charge. An aspect she liked about using sperm from an anonymous donor is that the children would be, in effect, hers alone. She felt no one else could tell her what to do with them. The son is now in his early 40's; the daughter is in her late 30's. They've never been told that Steve isn't their biological father.

Before she married Steve, Greta worked for a brief period as a secretary in an office in Manhattan. She enjoyed her job, and now looks back on it as the high point of her life. But even then, she felt she was an inferior worker — and physically unattractive because of her eye injury.

She thought no one would ever marry her. When she met Steve, he was already overweight, and not very good-looking otherwise. But, he was kind to her. There wasn't much chemistry, yet she felt she better marry him, fearing no one else would come along. Greta now regrets her marriage. But then, she regrets most of the rest of her life.

Though many people are unhappily married and have some other issues, Greta struggles even with everyday functioning. She yearns for friendship; yet she's afraid of people. She's lonely, scared, and depressed virtually all of the time.

During childhood, no one paid much attention to Greta. As noted, when her eye was injured, nothing was done about it until it was too late to save her sight in that eye. She was sexually abused, and nothing was done about that either — because she was too afraid to tell anyone.

Fear of Authority Figures

Helping Greta to work through her fears isn't going to be easy. So, in our initial sessions, I just listen to her. She's frightened by physicians, or anyone else she believes is in a position of authority. Her voice becomes childlike in their presence. For example, she's terrified of Dr. Kreuger, the psychiatrist who prescribes her medication. (I know Dr. Kreuger; he's a very nice man.)

Indeed, Greta has been very fearful her whole life. She'd only go for walks by herself, because going out with a friend caused her too much anxiety. She couldn't eat in a restaurant with a companion, because she'd feel like she's being watched and judged. Merely lifting a cup of coffee in front of a friend would frighten her. (So, she'd eat alone at diners and other inexpensive restaurants.)

Greta has a neighbor, Alice, who is very nosy. Whenever Greta opens her window blinds, she sees Alice looking out from her home. Alice is one of those New Yorkers who functions as an unofficial "block watcher" by spending much of her time peering out from her window. Greta is frightened by this — and very angry about it.

Greta would cry out during a session, "Why is she doing that?! Why is she watching me?!" It took a long time to help her realize that she can't change other people. That Alice has her own craziness. If Alice needs to look out her window, it's really not Greta's business. She doesn't have to get upset about someone else's neuroses.

Even now that she has made progress, other people's craziness is still a difficult issue for Greta. She has a tendency to ask, in a tone of distress, why people do what they do. We have painstakingly worked on trying to get her to keep herself "bounded" — because Greta worries about *everything*. I advise her to follow a suggestion that I learned from 12-Step programs: "One day at a time."

It's taken us years of hard work but, happily, Greta has definitely improved. When she initially came to me, she'd always been too dependent on others. There's a certain comfort in that role, because she didn't have to grow up and be self-reliant. She could be like an almost-helpless child.

Steve

Greta's husband, Steve, has diabetes. He was a doorman at a Manhattan hotel for many years, so he was a responsible breadwinner back then. But his diabetes has progressed to the point that he's no longer able to work. So they now live on Social Security and modest disability payments from his union. Yet, notwithstanding the big drop in their income, he runs up the monthly cable bill by watching porn nightly.

In spite of, or because of, his viewing habits, Steve doesn't share physical intimacy with Greta. I think she really misses this. He is by now about 400 pounds and eating everything in sight — clearly not arousing. It's a very unhappy existence for her.

But, Greta resists making any changes. For example, they have 2 TV's — yet *both* are in their living room. Steve doesn't watch just porn. He's a sports fan and loves watching televised games. He also likes to watch news, as well as police procedurals like *CSI* or *Law and Order: Special Victims Unit* (which focuses on violent sex crimes).

It's all very upsetting to Greta. She hates crime shows and sports. Instead, she likes comedies and love stories. Since they have both TV's in the same room, each showing a different program, they argue day and night. And yet, Greta still isn't willing to move her television into the bedroom. I've suggested headphones as an alternative, but Greta hasn't followed this suggestion either.

Because of his disability, for over a decade Steve has been home all day long, lying on the couch with his TV and his food. Greta waits on him hand and foot, fixing him breakfast, lunch, and dinner — with snacks in between.

Some of their furniture has already collapsed under his weight. She's fearful that he's going to also break the toilet, a sink, or the shower. When he goes into the kitchen, he sometimes knocks things onto the floor. She has to constantly be on "high alert" with Steve, as if he were a toddler.

As noted, they spend their days and evenings in the living room with 2 TV's, each tuned to a different channel. Steve watches his shows. Greta watches hers. They constantly argue:

"Turn down your TV, Steve."

"Shut up, Greta. Go to sleep."

"Don't tell me what to do. I'm not a child."

"Yes, you are. You're stupid."

Slow But Steady Progress

Although it's taken a long time, Greta has gotten much better. We've done some intensive work on her several chronic traumas, helping her identify her inner child. That little girl who is so hurt and angry, but feels powerless.

Sensing her own improvement, Greta has said to me, "It's amazing. I've seen several other therapists. All the others wrote me off as just crazy. No one else ever explained to me that there's a child inside of me who's been traumatized, and is reacting to certain triggers. I'm getting better. I feel stronger — like I have a voice now. I'm still not where I'd like to be, but I know that my life has changed."

For example, Greta has been doing more things on her own. She now enjoys shopping trips — even if it's just window-shopping — to the nicer stores. And, she's started going for walks in Central Park.

As mentioned, Greta had been unable to speak with Dr. Kreuger as one adult to another. She'd go 2 hours early to the mall where his office is located, then anxiously walk around the parking lot worrying about what he'd say to her. For example, if he was going to scold her for doing everything wrong in her dealings with Steve, etc.

By the time she'd see him, Greta would be so anxious that she couldn't think of the things she wanted to ask. She'd instead ask him in a childlike voice, "Doctor, is it okay if I have 1 more Xanax a day? If I do [this]? If I do [that]?"

I suggest to her, "Before leaving home, write your questions for Dr. Kreuger in a notebook, and bring it to your appointment. Also write a note to yourself: *I'm an adult. I'm allowed to ask questions. I have a right to know what my doctor thinks about my case — what his prognosis and treatment plan are.*

Though she's still a little anxious, it's nothing like before. Greta now goes to Dr. Kreuger's office without paralyzing fear. She can show up as an adult for her appointments.

She also recognizes when her inner traumatized child wants to be "in charge". This happens often. Trauma can keep an adult awkwardly stuck in their childhood years. But now, Greta realizes that she's an adult who can be in control and tell her inner child, *You aren't allowed to interfere in my life anymore.*

Going to the bank is something else Greta has had trouble with. In the past, she couldn't do a simple transaction, because she was so intimidated by the bank tellers. She looked at them as authority figures, and she felt unimportant by comparison. But, although Steve still writes the checks, he's too disabled to go to the bank anymore. So, Greta has been learning to do this on her own.

She's almost sure to outlive Steve. As noted, he has severe diabetes, and he weighs about 400 pounds. He has no energy, and can hardly breathe. Greta needs to be prepared for the day when she's likely to be living alone, and will have to write checks herself.

Also, Greta used to cut herself (because it made her feel less anxious). She still sometimes says she'd rather not be in this world anymore. But, these seem to be just idle no-tions. She's never spoken of a plan to actually end her life. Nevertheless, I've spoken to Dr. Kreuger about the issue. Neither of us thinks she'll attempt suicide, but, as will be seen, you never know.

The Group

In recent months, I've placed Greta in a group that I've been running with 3 or 4 other women in her age range. They've invited her to join them at a nearby diner after group is over. So Greta has started to form friendships. Though it's been a challenge, she's learned to eat in front of them.

Of particular note, there's a man at this diner who seems to have a romantic interest in Greta. He's started picking up the tab for her lunches. She's said to me, "I don't know what to do. Every time I go to the diner and order soup, this man pays for it!"

Aside from Steve, she has never experienced a man flirting with her. It has helped lift her spirit. She's started to think that maybe she's not as unattractive as she's been feeling her whole life.

Greta eventually discloses more details about her adoptive mother. She was a very tough, hard-working woman. While in her 70's, she once climbed up on her roof to nail down shingles. Greta isn't very athletic, and she's afraid of heights. She'd never climb a ladder to work on the roof. She's always admired her mother for being resourceful enough to do home repairs, plus a lot of other useful things. So, Greta has never felt able to live up to her mother's expectations.

In contrast with her mother's house, Greta's is falling apart. Steve can no longer do the work, but he doesn't want to pay anyone else. As noted, they live on Social Security and Steve's modest union benefits. All of their medical bills are charged on credit cards. After they pay the cable bill for Steve's porn habit, there isn't money left over for fixing up the house. But as long Steve has his porn, he's good.

As a result, their house is dilapidated. Heavy rains cause water to drip from their living room ceiling. The porch is badly sagging and, as mentioned, Steve's weight has already broken several things. Yet, nothing gets repaired.

I've suggested that Greta take the initiative. After all, the house is as much hers as his. If Steve can't or won't fix things in need of repair, she needs to pay a repairman to do it. Steve spends $100 to $120 a month on porn movies. This is enough to get a faucet or a leaking roof fixed. I've also suggested to her that she just shut off their cable account. But, Steve could call the cable company and turn it back on. And, she fears he'd retaliate in some way.

So Greta doesn't have an easy life. But, as mentioned, she's made some friends in the therapy group I've placed her in. She's visited one of the other members at her home. And, they've even made plans to have lunch together. Realistically, Greta probably won't ever be able to handle a large circle of friends, or lots of company. For Greta, friendship has to be in small doses.

But, at least she has found her voice, literally. She used to ask, in a tiny voice, if she's even allowed to say something. (We had to discuss why she felt the need to ask permission in the first place.) Now when she speaks, people can understand her, because she speaks in a normal adult voice.

She still takes a Xanax tablet daily for her anxiety, half in the morning and half at night. In my opinion, she'd probably do better with a *non*-addictive anti-anxiety drug, or an SSRI for depression. But, she doesn't want to try, because she has so much difficulty with any kind of change.

Admittedly, she does have some valid reasons to be anxious. It's scary to be over 70 with no savings, and a very ill husband who doesn't care about anything anymore.

Greta's adult children aren't there for her either. They're busy living their own lives and hardly ever visit, or even call. And, she has no grandchildren.

To sum up: This may be as good as it gets for Greta. But she's in a lot better shape than a dozen years ago, when she'd come to my office literally shaking with fear. Nowadays, she makes some time just for herself. She leaves

Steve at home and goes for walks. She's also started doing some routine exercises. I've shown her a few stretches and other gentle exercises she can do.

Greta's case is one of the toughest I've worked on. Her previous therapists gave up trying to help her. She's not young, it took awhile to get her to talk about her past issues, and after all this time, her insurance plan still pays me only $20 per session. Because of the money Steve spends on porn, she can't afford a co-pay.

Yet, Greta *has* made progress. Instead of seeing her every week, I now see her once every 2 weeks. She's amazed that it has taken almost her whole life to undo all the tangled stuff from her childhood that she carried around for so long. But, Greta tells me, she now feels very different than when we began.

𝕮leaning 𝕳ouse

"I'm looking for a gunman who'll kill me," Violet says in our 1st session, because she has no reason to live. She was sexually abused from early childhood until age 11. Now 53, she has no money saved, she's always anxious — at times panicked — and so she wants to die.

Violet was already suffering from anxiety back when she worked as a receptionist/secretary at the original World Trade Center. After 9/11, her anxiety became unbearable. When riding the subway to work, she kept imagining the train would get stuck in the tunnel under the East River.

So, Violet quit her job at WTC, and became a home health aide in Queens, assisting a man in his 80's. Though it's against the rules of the agency she works for, she's now living in his home, because she can't afford NYC rents on the pay she earns from the agency.

When Violet comes for her 1st appointment, we make a verbal contract that I'll work with her if she'll agree to not harm herself. She agrees, and we begin.

Childhood Abuse

Violet was born in the Caribbean, but she has been in New York for about 30 years. During her early childhood, her father abused her sexually. And, he impregnated a lover while Violet's mother was pregnant with another of his children. Alcoholism was also present in her family.

When Violet was 3, her mother, who was overwhelmed by her own issues left Violet with an aunt who raised her to age 12. The aunt's husband also repeatedly violated Violet. By the time she was 8, Violet already wanted to kill herself, to escape the sexual abuse.

The aunt was good to her, and met her basic needs, but this aunt had serious medical problems. So when Violet was 12, she was taken to another aunt's house to be raised. The 2nd aunt fed Violet and made sure she got a good education during this period. But this aunt was cold and show-ed her no affection. Violet was afraid to go to sleep at night, because that's when she was abused again. So, at 13 she attempted suicide by overdosing on pills. Fortunately, a friend intervened and took her to a hospital, where Violet's life was saved.

She went back to living at her mother's house at the age of 16. Violet now had 7 siblings — 5 from her father and 2 from a step-father who had entered the picture.

Thus, her various caretakers were too busy to attend to Violet's needs as a child. No one was there to protect her.

The house her family was then living in burned down, because someone torched a nearby house, and the fire spread to her house. Afterward, Violet bounced around from one relative's household to another.

An uncle agreed to pay for her continued schooling. But when she went to his house to iron his laundry, he raped her. Violet felt she had a sign on her that read, *Abuse Me.*

A few years ago, she was in a romantic relationship with a man she trusted completely. But after a year of dating, she found out he was lying when he said he's single. She felt deeply hurt by his betrayal, and hasn't dated anyone since.

Plus, in 2000, she almost died after having intestinal surgery.

EMDR

But in spite of all her misfortunes, Violet does have some things going for her. She's pretty, looks younger than her age, and is always smartly dressed. She used to run track and field (an interest she shared with the man she dated), and she remains in good shape. She's very religious, and her church is a source of consolation and friendship. Still, living alone in New York has been very hard for her.

As she becomes more stable during the course of treatment, we start to do EMDR (eye movement desensitization and re-processing). In EMDR, the client moves her eyes laterally, following the therapist's index and middle fingers while moving her arms, also laterally. It's the lateral eye movement that dislodges the trauma in the brain, reprocesses it, and then deletes it for good.

She struggles at first, but soon responds very well to EM-DR. We're able to address significant issues from her childhood, and the memories that are so troubling for her.

Violet is in treatment with me for over 2 years. Little by little, she starts to feel better. We talk about what some of her goals might be. Her dream is to have her own house cleaning business. She loves cleaning, and experiences it as a form of self-therapy.

A member of her church who lives in Hawaii invites Violet to stay with her. Violet relocates there in 2013, but stays in touch with me by texting or calling every so often. She's very happy in Hawaii, and is living her best life there. She starts her own cleaning business, as she had planned, and it does really well.

In 2016, however, she calls to say she'll be moving to Panama to take care of an elderly aunt who lives there. Although Violet loves her cleaning business — it's shown her she can be successful — it's now time for her to care for her aunt. She moves to Panama late that year.

Recently, her aunt comes to NYC for a surgical procedure, and Violet accompanies her. While her aunt is recuperating in the hospital, Violet and I get together for dinner. She tells me that because of my help, she's finally happy. She had no hope when she first came to me. She'd had enough of life, and just wanted to die. But by working together on her issues, she's found hope and peace, and is now living a contented life.

Instant Gratification

Roger has his own successful business, a beautiful wife and family, and an expensive home. Yet, he's severely depressed. He seeks my help after more than a year of not finding relief from different anti-depressant medications.

He has over 10 years' sobriety in AA, but has meanwhile become a sex addict (substituting one source of instant gratification for another). He's been finding women to join in threesomes with his wife, Carla. Roger isn't discreet about it. Women who live and work in their neighborhood are among those he tries to recruit. So he's exposed his family to the inevitable gossip.

However, when Carla and I have a solo session, she tells me she doesn't want to be involved with this lifestyle anymore. She wants to take a different path entirely. In fact, she wants to leave Roger — though not while he's still going through this major depression. She's assured him she won't abandon him until he gets better. She wants to continue to be his good friend, but no longer his wife.

Unfortunately, as with the anti-depressants he's been taking, Roger doesn't do well in treatment with me either. I even try sending him to practitioners of alternative treatments. But, he still doesn't get the quick results he wants.

By doing his own internet research, Roger learns about transcranial magnetic stimulation (TMS). He travels to an out-of-state clinic that offers this procedure. The clinic takes him off all meds, and applies TMS. Like virtually every other form of treatment, whether for a mental or physical problem, not every patient responds well. Unfortunately, Roger gets no relief from TMS. The clinic tells him that his only remaining option is electroconvulsive therapy (ie, shock therapy). Roger doesn't want to go that route.

Instead, he wants the instant gratification he once had with alcohol and later with sex. He doesn't want to do the long-term work of uncovering underlying issues and really addressing them. Medications haven't lifted his depression, nor have various other treatments. (He's tried more than I've mentioned.) The TMS clinic's webpage raised his hopes again that there's a quick fix. When TMS doesn't deliver it, Roger feels crushed.

I speak to him on the phone on Friday evening after he gets back to New York. He voices his despair that TMS hasn't helped him. I ask him if he's safe — if he's thinking of hurting himself. He replies that he wouldn't do anything like that, especially since one of his kids is still a child. He'd never damage his child that way.

Although we've already made an appointment for Monday, to be on the safe side I offer him a next-day appointment instead. He assures me he'll be okay until Monday.

However, on Monday he neither shows up nor calls to cancel. The next day, I get a call from a mutual acquaintance who related that at lunchtime the day before, Roger sent out his secretary to bring back lunch for the 2 of them. When she got back, she found that Roger had committed suicide by shooting himself in the head.

In a dark sense, Roger finally got the instant gratification he was seeking. Naturally, his family has suffered the most, but I too am very upset by this, as any therapist would be.

Sometimes our best efforts fail to bring about the change a person comes to us for.

Reunited And It Feels So Good

Shaunda is a 6-year-old in foster care when she becomes my client at New York Family. As her social worker, I sometimes take her shopping. Early on, Shaunda would ask me what I want — so she could steal it for me.

She reveals that when she'd shop with her mother, she'd steal whatever her mother wanted. (Her mother is a drug addict.) I explain to her that she needn't steal anymore.

Much of her family still lives in the American South, but her mother is now in New York City. Shaunda has an older brother who is also in foster care. She herself came into foster care when her mother had another baby. This younger sibling, a girl, is now in foster care too.

Though only 6, Shaunda has already lived in 3 or 4 different foster homes. When I meet her, she's living in an apartment-like diagnostic unit at New York Family. She's very smart, people like her, and she has a number of other strengths. But, she's also strong-willed and a little bit wild. (She's gone through a lot for someone so young.)

I get in touch with her birth mother, who by this time is in a drug rehab facility in uptown Manhattan. From time to time, I take Shaunda there to visit her mom.

I also make it a point to locate and contact Shaunda's Aunt Cheryl, who still lives in the South. She had no idea that Shaunda is in the NYC foster care system.

Cheryl's husband is career military. For a few years, they were living in Germany, where he was stationed. They lost track of Shaunda's mother, because she was doing crack cocaine, and was basically unavailable.

When Cheryl learns Shaunda is in foster care, she says that of course she and her husband want to adopt Shaunda.

I'm involved with the whole process. I make the arrangements, including their hotel stay, for the aunt and uncle to come to NYC (with their son) to meet Shaunda. And I check to be sure things are going smoothly while they're here.

They come to NYC to visit Shaunda a couple of times, and all goes well. Eventually Shaunda is formally adopted by her aunt and uncle, and is raised by them in the South.

For a time, I don't hear from her. Then one day, about a decade ago, Shaunda calls me, having gotten my contact information from Google. (She's so excited she has found me!)

Shaunda tells me she's won the Teenager of the Year Award in the city where she now lives. She's been written up in the local newspaper for an essay she wrote about her life: starting out as an abused and neglected child in foster care, eventually being adopted, doing well in school, graduating with honors, and being accepted at a good college. Shaunda thanks me for locating her Aunt Cheryl, because otherwise they wouldn't have been reunited.

Back when she was my client, I could've thought, *She's in foster care and I'm already overworked (like everyone else there), so I don't have the time to find her extended family.*

But instead, I put a lot of effort into her case. When I left New York Family in 2000, the adoption had been finalized. I was glad the process was completed while I was still there, so that I could've provided more help, if it'd been needed.

Shaunda keeps me up to date by sending messages and emails from time to time. She recently wrote a beautiful note about how my work really made a big difference in her life. And, she invited me to her college graduation. I wasn't able to go, but one day she might come and visit me. Or, who knows, maybe I'll go down South to visit her.

These days, Shaunda is doing really well. She has a steady job and her own apartment. She continues to have a great relationship with her adoptive family, and now has a good bond with her mom, who seems to have stayed in recovery. She's gotten together with her younger sister (who has been adopted by another family), and she's also in touch with her brother.

In sum, all the pieces seem to have come together for Shaunda.

Mother and Son Disunion

Bobby Joe and Wanda grow up in the South. They meet when both are in the US military. At that time, Wanda is a young adult, and Bobby Joe is 15 years older. He's very self-controlled, while she's still unsure of herself — and susceptible to crying in stressful situations. Bobby Joe provides Wanda with steady emotional support, and they eventually marry.

However, 2 years after the birth of Beau, their only child together, they divorce. The court grants them joint custody. So, although Beau continues to live with his father, Wanda has substantial visitation rights.

Jared

But after she remarries, Wanda lives with her new husband, Jared, in a different state. So she visits Beau much less frequently, from when Beau's 2 until he's 4. However, at age 3, Beau visits Wanda and Jared. When he returns, Beau tells Bobby Joe that he doesn't want to visit them again, because Jared touched him inappropriately.

Bobby Joe has child protection services investigate. Beau relates to them the inappropriate touching, and that Jared told him that this was a "secret" he shouldn't tell anyone. Wanda, for her part, says that Jared merely gave Beau a sugary treat he shouldn't have been having before a meal, and that's why Jared told Beau not to tell anyone.

A medical examination doesn't find physical evidence of molestation, so no legal charges are brought against Jared. Nevertheless, the authorities are sufficiently persuaded by Beau's credibility that sole custody over him is given to Bobby Joe. Wanda's visitation rights are greatly restricted, and even then, only in the presence of adult supervision. Jared is forbidden to have any contact with Beau at all.

Beau's New Mom

Sometime later, Bobby Joe meets Bonita online. She lives in NYC, having immigrated to the US 30 years earlier. Of great importance to Bobby Joe, Bonita has her act together. They marry, and he and Beau move to NYC to live with her. Bonita and Beau soon grow very close.

Meanwhile, Jared gets a job in a New England state. Wanda is now close enough to visit Beau in NYC regularly. This is in addition to their mid-week Skype call, and a regular phone call on weekends (both court-mandated).

By this time, Bobby Joe is living on disability payments from the military. In NYC, it's barely enough to meet the family's needs. So, Bobby Joe and Bonita decide to relocate to the South, where a dollar goes further. Wanda reacts to their plan by filing a lawsuit in NYC's Family Court, seeking to block the move on the ground that it would effectively deny her visitation rights with Beau.

Sessions

The Family Court judge initially sympathizes with Wanda. It's at this point that Bobby Joe and Beau first come to me. Over the course of a year, I have joint sessions with Bobby Joe and Beau, and also solo sessions with each of them. Bobby Joe, at first out of his own pocket and later through military benefits, pays for all of these sessions. (It's not until 6 months have passed that the VA starts to reimburse me for the visits. Until then, I accept $40 per session.)

Wanda says she can't afford to pay anything, so at first I see her only in family sessions. But eventually the judge orders her to have solo sessions too. I charge her $40 also.

It's clear from the start that Beau simply doesn't want Wanda in his life at this stage of his development. He's conflicted about this, because his Christian faith requires that he respect her. But, although aware she gave birth to him, he doesn't *experience* Wanda as his mother. Bonita is the one he has these feelings for.

Beau's Bad Memories

Beau hasn't forgotten Wanda sided with Jared after Jared violated him. Overall, she hasn't been in his life very much, even for special events like Christmas or his birthday.

He tells me the only things she's ever bought for him are novelty items from a 99¢ store, which feels to him like a slap in the face. Bobby Joe is the one who's paid for anything of consequence. Overall, Beau feels that Wanda abandoned him when he needed her most, and now she's just interfering in his life.

So, the contacts with Wanda that the court has required — Skype calls, regular phone calls, in-person visits — have been an ordeal for Beau. When they get together, she wants to do things like take him to a museum and other venues where they will have opportunities to interact. Beau would rather do things that enable him to tune her out — like shoot paintballs.

There isn't anything he wants to share with her during the midweek Skype call and the weekend phone call. For him these calls, besides being awkward in themselves, are time that isn't available for schoolwork or leisure.

Upon meeting Beau in session, I find him to be smart, articulate, and surprisingly insightful for someone who isn't quite yet a teenager. Tellingly, he doesn't refer to Wanda as "my mother", but instead simply as "Wanda".

Although he's previously been well behaved, Beau has recently begun acting out in school. Kid stuff — nothing serious. But still, a sign that he's having increasing difficulty coping with the stress he experiences in being forced to interact with Wanda.

Wanda

I first meet Wanda in an informal setting away from my office. She seems very skillful at managing impressions. Wanda takes no responsibility for Beau not wanting to relate to her. She places all of the blame on Bobby Joe, and expresses confidence that in time Beau will warm up to her.

Beau hasn't candidly told Wanda how he feels about her. He's afraid she'll silence him, and then launch into a big lecture. Over the course of our sessions, I give him the confidence to be frank with her — within the safety of my office.

It's in a session with the 2 of them that Beau tells Wanda how he really feels. It's pretty dramatic to watch this boy, still only 12, pacing back and forth as if he were a trial attorney cross-examining a hostile witness. Beau recites a list of times she hasn't been there for him. At one point he asks, "Have you ever bought me a pair of pants?!" Hearing Beau speak to her this way, especially in front of another person, must have been very difficult for Wanda, as it would be for any mother.

During the almost year-long period I work with this family, I have to keep in mind my feelings about having been abandoned by my own mother. I strive to avoid countertransference, which in this case would be my over-identifying with Beau, to the detriment of being fair to Wanda.

The Court's Decision

In the course of their treatment, I spend a lot of time writing reports and letters to the relevant legal authorities. In my final report to the Family Court judge, I indicate that at this time in his life Beau clearly doesn't want to have a mother-son relationship with Wanda.

Now approaching puberty, Beau has grown closer to his father, as a male role model (which, needless to say, would be out of the question with Jared). If there is ever to be a thaw in Beau's feelings toward Wanda, this isn't the right time to force him to be with her. I strongly recommend that Beau be allowed to find his own way for now, and that Bobby Joe's plan to move his family back to the South not be interfered with further.

In the Family Court judge's final ruling, she allows the move, and reduces Beau's mandated contact time with Wanda to 2 phone calls per month.

A Letter From Beau

Afterward, I receive a note from Beau, expressing his gratitude. He writes, in part, "Thank you for what you did for me...You helped me overcome this mountain of stressfulness...No matter what happened you stuck by me in those hard times, you understood how I felt and what I was going through...I've talked to other therapists and none of them have helped me as much as you did."

Like many counselors, I sometimes wonder if the work I do is actually helping people. I think I've helped Beau.

Feeling Grateful

Thank you, God. I've come a long way from a dark, lonely, and cold place, feeling the world and everyone in it had forgotten me and my children. I no longer have to choose between having sex for money or watching my children go hungry. I no longer have to be poor and isolated. I feel very blessed and grateful.

www.ingramcontent.com/pod-product-compliance
Lightning Source LLC
Chambersburg PA
CBHW070954040426
42443CB00007B/503